T0274235

Wake Up to Love

Wake Up to Love

Meditations to Start Your Day

Nikki Walton

HarperOne
An Imprint of HarperCollinsPublishers

FIRST EDITION

Designed by Janet Evans-Scanlon

Part opener illustrations © Gia Walton
Heart used throughout © OceanArt/stock.adobe.com
Texture used throughout © kanpisut/stock.adobe.com
Art on pages 8 and 349 © Dorothy Art/stock.adobe.com

Library of Congress Cataloging-in-Publication Data has been applied for.

ISBN 978-0-06-341574-4

24 25 26 27 28 LBC 5 4 3 2 1

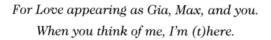

For Love appearing as Gia, Max, and you.
When you think of me, I'm (t)here.

"Wake up and learn of three things as one, and one as three."
_____

WILLIAM HENRY QUOTING *THE BOOK OF LOVE*

This isn't a book.
You are not a person.
Here is not "here."
This is not "now."
This is Love.
And you are that Love.

I am not a book.
I am The Vibration,
The Comforter,
Divine Love in form.
I Am always in the midst of you,
but your call,
your sincere desire for help,
has caused Me to appear this way.
Before reading any further,
close and place Me before you.
Looking at what appears to be only a book,
without blinking,
eyes wide open,
eyebrows raised,
feel My Silence rise within you.
I see the miracles in you.
Begin.

CONTENTS

Love Is All You Need

When I sit in the morning to chant or pray the rosary,
I am sitting down to feel Love.
When I am doing Yoga or Pranayama, I am doing it to feel Love.
When I do any spiritual practice, I am doing it only as a way to feel Love.
The practice will get you, in the words of the Hindu guru Neem Karoli
Baba (Maharajji), "in the room with God."
But only Love will keep you (t)here.
Everything I do,
I do for Love—
to remember It,
to feel It,
to know It as my Self.

"IS THIS LOVE ENOUGH?"

Frustrated, I wrote those words down in my journal.

It wasn't one I kept daily; I seemed to reach for it only when life made me feel helpless. I had been practicing Divine Love for five years at that point, meaning I was doing my best not to take a breath, take a step, or speak a word until inner Love was felt, as if I were holding It. As if Love were a lit candle in my trembling hands, in a dark and unfamiliar place, with no extra matches. I could see only the next step in front of me, and I had to move slowly, consciously, thoughtlessly (silently), and yet faithfully to keep from being lost in the dark. This little flame felt unstable, fragile, conditional, but that was all me. I was the wavering one. It never flickered. It doesn't go out.

I experienced this Love as a felt oneness with everything. The world still looked the same, but there was a simultaneous awareness that only Love is here, appearing as "me" and everything "I" see. Whether I was getting news of a delayed flight, of a sick family member, or that a long-awaited contract had come through, I would immediately "turn" to Love. I say "turn" because it would feel like I would turn back on myself, turn to myself, like the attention that was going out, seeing out, would see "in." But my eyes couldn't look back on themselves—instead, I would instantly hear Silence instead of thoughts. And in that loud inner Silence (no matter how noisy the outer environment), I'd find the same sweetness that manifested sometimes as a sense of relief or relaxation and at other times as an ecstatic joy that would make me want to hug the world. Always pleasant. Always here. Often forgotten. Usually covered over by thoughts. This simple awareness of Love would appear as effortlessly rebooked flights with no lost time, healings, material and spiritual abundance, and new opportunities—the Good life, a God life (they are one in the same). It still does—miracles flow like breath. This is the new normal.

> "Just as the hem of Jesus' garment flowed healing virtue
> (Matthew 9:20; 14:36), so even the borders of the inner
> kingdom flow with a glory impossible to describe—
> but very easy to experience."
>
> ABBOT GEORGE BURKE,
> *THE GOSPEL OF THOMAS FOR AWAKENING*

I am turning to It again as these words appear. This back-and-forth, stress/release, tension/relaxation, ease/hardship, not conscious of

Love/Love-Conscious went on for years as if I were tap dancing at a threshold—the world on one side (often experienced as hell), heaven on the other. Why would I keep visiting hell if heaven was an option? How could I know for sure that this Love I was feeling, being, was enough? What did I mean by "enough"? Enough to take me all the way, or to dissolve "me" in Enlightenment? Enough to help me accomplish my lofty worldly goals?

I didn't have to wait long for answers. Within three days, a spontaneous phone call with a spiritual conference organizer named Swaady led to an unforeseen opportunity. Within the week, I'd be in South Africa (by way of St. Louis, Missouri), onstage with Coldplay, throwing out Love buttons into a stadium full of concertgoers, speaking on my first panel about Love-Consciousness, and meeting Oprah. It was a wild manifestation. My flight was delayed; bag got lost; I made it to South Africa with two hours to spare to get to Oprah's event. I had to buy clothes and underwear at the airport (there was a Woolworth's on-site). The VIP lounge was full of people, and when I saw the backstage hospitality suite out of the corner of my eye, I entered as I if I was supposed to be there! The rest is history, but it's still fun to tell it.

When I booked the flight, I was told about the Global Citizen Festival happening that same weekend but also made aware that the tickets were sold out. The spiritual conference speakers couldn't attend or meet any of the headliners. I didn't mind; I just knew I needed to be there, on the ground. Not even twenty-four hours later, I reached out to Dr. Sadeghi, a holistic doctor in California, to thank him for sending me a box of books and Love buttons months before (which I had just received because I'd finally made the once-a-quarter trip to my post office box), apologizing for the delay and sharing that I'd reach out when I got back from South Africa. He wrote back immediately asking if I was going to the Global Citizen Festival. I told him that I wasn't and I'd be in Johannesburg at a different event. He replied, "You're the luckiest woman in the world. Call me." He sent his number and I called immediately. He told me about his nonprofit organization's major campaign with Chris Martin of Coldplay ("Believe in Love") and how he was supposed to be at the festival to do the opening prayer and get footage for his social media channels. He couldn't make it, and he wanted to send me some Love buttons to take with me to pass out. I reminded him that he had already sent more than two hundred! We were good to go! He supplied me with VIP tickets and even backstage passes to every event.

I asked Oprah whether her quote "I define joy as a sustained sense of well-being and internal peace—a connection to what matters" was just flowery language or a felt experience, and before leaning in for the selfie I'd requested, she touched her hand to her chest, over her heart, and said, "It's absolutely a feeling I sustain." And I could feel It sustaining me.

It was Love's appearance as a spontaneous, last-minute trip to South Africa that not only solidified my faith in Love (by feeding me, transporting me, and introducing me to It appearing as other spiritual beings) but also helped me begin this new career. It was remaking my inner and outer worlds—melding the two. It's not that being Love inside attracts good things outside—there is no outside! Love is the GoOD thing and appears as the good things. It's everything. And as the great Indian Hindu mystic Sri Ramakrishna said, either the water is boiling or it's not. Either you're Love-conscious or you're not. And at that moment, I made an intention to not step out of the Kingdom, to not cross back over that threshold for anything. I am Love-Conscious. God-Conscious. I am That, I Am. And You are, too. I invite you to see It.

Bow back into God,
back into your Shelter,
like you're ducking under the doorframe back inside where it's quiet,
where there is no world, nothing to solve, nothing to fix, nothing
to think about.
This is your default setting.

I write this at my bedroom window, looking out at the Gulf of Mexico, with a top podcast about Love, sipping a cup of Love—the cappuccino I learned to make at home after my most recent spiritual pilgrimage to Assisi, Italy. Life is GoOD.

It's Love.
And It speaks.
When I know who I Am,
I call It Me;
when I want to pretend there's two,
I call It Maharajji,
Mataji,
Jesus,
Krishna,
or Our Lady, the Divine Mother.
*But It's always just **the Christ**.*
Just Love.
Just the "I Am."

That selfsame Spirit animated, pervaded, and appeared as all of those great beings.

It is looking out at these words from that body's eyes, from the eyes of that body you call yours, appearing as "you"; it's looking out from here, appearing as "me."

"The blessing God has for you is where He is, and He is with you."

———————

DERRIKA DANIELLE
(@THEREALSWEETSPOT ON INSTAGRAM)

Every morning, It wakes this body up and sits it down at the microphone. I try to find words. But nothing comes. I scroll through quotes on my phone (I have a gazillion screenshots and pics), but they're like random pieces of seven different thousand-piece puzzles. But then the "turning" happens, the Silence is heard, and the Love I am feeling becomes words. The Word becomes the words, the relevant quotes are triggered and spoken, and another episode is completed. I just have to show up.

You just have to show up.

You show up and let Love show you what's here.

Words, podcast episodes, books are here where I appear to be. And I can feel that you have a hunch what is waiting to be uncovered, unfolded (t)here, where you appear to be. Don't be overwhelmed, don't be doubtful; just know. Knowing is silent. It's loving.

Each morning, you'll come here and find Love waiting for you with a fresh message to help you remember who you are, to Love Its creation into being, through you.

Are you ready?

Everything brought you to this moment,
for you to hear this message,
for you to receive this certainty,
before you go back out into the appearance, the field of uncertainty.
For you to feel this confidence,
to be this Confidence,
even while you appear to be unsure,
even while in the storyline, you're doubting, you're stumbling,
you're falling.
In your Heart, simultaneously, there's a knowing that you're
carried.
That all you have to do is relax and allow,
let go and receive.
Stand up and know you're not alone,
know that you have Me by your side,
in front of you,
in back of you,
within your Heart—
that's My Home.
I'm always within
and I Am all you need.
The "I Am," this felt Love, the way you know you're alive,
is all you need.

You Are Called to Rise

"Jesus said, 'Blessed is he who came into being before he
came into being.'"

———————

ABBOT GEORGE BURKE,
THE GOSPEL OF THOMAS FOR AWAKENING

"Also you shall testify, that from the beginning You have
been with Me."

———————

JESUS (JOHN 15:27), VICTOR N. ALEXANDER,
ARAMAIC SCRIPTURE

WHO I AM

I Am who You were before you were born,
who You still are and always will be.
I appear to take birth,
to take shape,
but I am beyond birth and death,
beyond all shapes,
colors,
gender,
age,
names,
and words.
I existed before language,
before every Sound.
I Am the Love.
The Womb.
The Mother and the Son.
The Silence and the Tolling,
this fine Ringing in your Right Ear.
The Caller, the Calling, and the Called.
It's Your Time.
Listen . . .
FEEL.
Rise.
Receive these messages as wake-up calls,
as reminder texts that you're Love(d).
Each morning you will come to know Me better,
by practicing My Presence—
feeling Love even where you feel pain,
catching Me smiling at you from every face,

feeling the wind as My breath,
smelling the rose as My fragrance,
enjoying the sun's warmth as My embrace.
Feeling your heartbeat as Mine.
I Am reading these words.
I wrote them, also,
Everything is Me and yet Nothing Is.
As you come to know this,
Nothing will be the same.
Love changes everything.

God is Love and Love is God. It is Formless and yet appears in and as form. It knows no opposite, needs no subject, and can't be generated, only noticed and lived. It's the Original Feeling that, when forgotten, appears as conditional feelings.

LOVE in the World's Great Religions:

Christianity: "Beloved, let us love one another, for love is of God; and everyone that loveth is born of God, and knoweth God. He that loveth not, knoweth not God, for God is Love."

Confucianism: "To love all men is the greatest benevolence."

Buddhism: "Let a man cultivate towards the whole world a heart of love."

Hinduism: "One can best worship the Lord through love."

Islam: "Love is this, that thou shouldst account thyself very little and God very great."

Taoism: "Heaven arms with Love those it would not see destroyed."

Sikhism: "God will regenerate those in whose hearts there is Love."

Judaism: "Thou shalt love the Lord thy God with all thy heart and thy neighbor as thyself."

Jainism: "The days are of most profit to him who acts in Love."

Zoroastrianism: "Man is the beloved of the Lord and should love him in return."

Baha'i: "Love Me that I may love thee. If thou lovest Me not, My love can no wise reach thee."

Shinto: "Love is the representative of the Lord."

RAM DASS, *BE HERE NOW*

WHY I'M HERE

Whether you're in a relationship or not, you're still looking for Love.
You may feel it as the spark you think you've lost,
or as loneliness, even when others are around.
Everyone else seems to have it together,
seems to get it
But not you.
You've always felt different.
Like an observer,

a visitor,

an outsider,

a pretender.

Only feigning happiness.

Playing human.

Fake smiling.

And you've only grown more introverted,

even as you appear more extroverted.

You prefer solitude,

and yet you also long for True Connection.

That's why I'm here.

You've been staring down at that phone for so long,

looking for Me out there,

as relief from boredom,

as more security,

as success,

as purpose,

as new Love,

but I've been right here.

Waiting for you to look up.

To look in.

And then to look back out, lovingly, as Me.

When you're in touch with Me,

you are naturally in touch with Everything and Everyone,

even those you feel guilty for falling out of touch with.

Tending to Our relationship will mend and grow all others.

But understanding Our relationship,

recognizing that there is no "relationship,"

that there's only One of Us,

will make everything new.

"Behold, I make all things new."

_____

REVELATION 21:5, NKJV

How to Read *Wake Up to Love*

"Consciousness equals
Energy =
Love =
Awareness =
Light =
Wisdom =
Beauty =
Truth =
Purity.
It's all the same trip
It's all the same
Any trip you want to take
leads to the same place"

———————

RAM DASS, *BE HERE NOW*

"He [Bawa Muhaiyaddeen] came in a dream once. He was teaching me to take tiny little sips out of a glass of water, I think. So tiny, like a little bee or butterfly drinking. And I said, 'What does this mean?' And he says, 'You want to be wise too quickly. Just take one sip of wisdom and assimilate that.' So that was good advice. Don't be in a hurry with the wisdom. Just take it—don't get greedy with it."

COLEMAN BARKS

This collection of Love Letters from your Self to your Self is meant to be read over the course of a year, one Practice per week. The Indivisible has been divided into five parts: Waking Up to Love, Sustaining Love, Being Love, Spreading Love, and The Fruit of Love. Until the time comes that you feel this Love constantly, you can use these practices and pick the ones that work the best, that are the most effective; and that will change from day to day. And so I'll give you a full tool kit to pull from.

Part One: Waking Up to Love contains fifteen practices that teach you how to turn to Love on demand. How to feel It instantly, no matter what. You'll find that Love is always here to feel; you can just sit up into It or breathe, sway, or rock back into It. You can intentionally smile your way into It or dance, praise, pray, sing, bow, and thank your way back in. Two seconds to Love, or, rather, two seconds to the recognition of Love.

Note: Love is One. There isn't a second, separate "you" feeling the perception of Love, but we can start here! The moment you feel Love, you are enlightened; you know by feeling, only Love is here.

Part Two: Sustaining Love shares sixteen practices for learning to "hold" this Real Happiness (the kind that doesn't have an opposite, the kind that's not dependent on your outer circumstances) while letting go of everything else. And when you finally let go of the one who thinks she needs to "let go," you'll find that Love has been holding you all along. Carrying you. Providing for you. Sustaining you. This is the real Ceaseless Prayer: Constant awareness of Silence, of Love, of God. Constant awareness of Grace. You no longer need prayer: you are Prayer. You are the Miracle.

> "This is not about becoming a more Aware
> person than the person next to you.
> This is about realizing you are not a person,
> there is no person next to you,
> and there is nothing other than Awareness."
>
> ———————
>
> **PAT NOLAN**

Part Three: Being Love delivers eighteen practices to help you trust and finally surrender to Love. To let It in, to breathe It out, to be baptized in and reborn of the Spirit. These pointings will dissolve "you" into You, bringing the one to the One, Love to Love, so that you may say from direct experience, "Only Love is Here." And that this Love is "the Way, the Truth, and the Life," the path and the destination. "*The practice and the reward*" (as my friend Sitaram Dass put it in his book *From and for God*). This felt-Love, God's Presence, begins to replace the appearance, the scene—the people, places, and things that you see. Where you see and experience the many, you'll feel only the One. You feel Love where you see the world. You feel Love where you see your body, your neighbor, your coworker. You're no longer fooled. You no longer judge by appearances. It's a simultaneous awareness that you wake up as, and not over the course of months or years but Now and Now and Now until even "Now" is seen as the concept it is. You will know and be the Form-less while still appearing as form, as that person. Your Consciousness will be enlightened. Enlivened. You will be in the world but not of it. You will be the Christed One as you exist in and as this new, risen way, on Earth, as you are in heaven. These practices aim "to keep you knowing what you are, while what you are not is present," as Shri Amritji said during a talk I attended at his ashram. Love becomes louder and more pronounced than that body, mind, and everything else (no matter what you're tasting, seeing, hearing, smelling, touching, thinking—Love is felt, too, and more); it fills you and begins to spill over. It begins to spread, spontaneously, powerfully.

You go from trusting in a God out there,
to trusting God as a presence inside
(though still separate from yourself),
to knowing It as your Self.
When you finally recognize that It is You,
that's true Trust.
Real Love,
Security, finally.

"One Knowing and Feeling behind everything."

NEIL DOUGLAS-KLOTZ,
REVELATIONS OF THE ARAMAIC JESUS

"Abide in Awareness with no illusion of person. You will be instantly free and at peace."

ASHTAVAKRA GITA

Part Four: Spreading Love will take you further into the appearance, into your worldly purpose and successful work, God's dream for you, while maintaining awareness as Love. My podcast, *GoOD Mornings with CurlyNikki*, is a direct manifestation of this, and it holds me in Love as I hold you. In Don Steven's book *The Awakener of the Age*, Meher Baba is quoted as saying, "No amount of prayer or meditation can do what helping others can do." You'll practice ways to extend, serve, support, feed, and Love others as your Self. Because the seeming others are your Self. Serving the world is how you serve God. Loving the rest of your Self is how you Love God. You may still see people you would prefer not to hang around, but your Love of Love transcends your human preferences and disagreements. You love the Love that is appearing as "difficult" people. You feel the Truth of them, and sometimes just that will wake them up to that Truth, too. In fact, it's your job as the Saint you are (and are becoming) to see only the highest, to look for God in every pair of eyes, beyond every frown and scary headline. You can no longer turn a blind eye. Just because a problem appears to be on the other side of the world, that doesn't mean you can tune it out. Everything you see becomes your responsibility to enlighten. To be Silent-Love aware of the seeming problem. Knowing that a solution will soon follow. Knowing that sometimes, that body you call yours will be involved in the solution, in the required action, and at other times, You, this Awareness, will simply be the catalyst that will engage seeming others. From this day forth, no matter your career, your real job is Love.

Work with each practice for one week. The longer reading is for the mind; the practice is for the Soul and can be applied successfully, immediately, and repeatedly—I recommend repeating the practices daily. Love can always be felt, known, in this "holy instant" (a term popularized with *A Course in Miracles*). Take it one holy instant at a time, consistently applying the practice, and you'll look up at God and finally see It. You're always looking at It, but you see these words, you see this book, you see those hands, that furniture, or that tree or sky, yet you're looking at God and seeing those things, misperceiving God as things. Soon (and that "soon" will be experienced as "now") you'll see God, Love, as It really is, as You really are.

Alternatively, you can flip to any page and let Love show you how It wants to be practiced in that moment. Share with your GoOD friends and rise in Love together as One!

You'll notice that the parts of this book are mightily uneven, but that's kinda how the process goes—you start off with all of these practices, all of this effort, and then it slowly trickles down into effortless effort; the practices that are left can barely even be called that. And only You are left—silent, abundant, naked, perfect—Eden, the Original State.

> "How many minutes, hours and days have you spent in your lives being happy from within? Those are the only moments you have really lived life."
>
> ———
>
> **SRI SRI RAVI SHANKAR**

Part Five: The Fruit of Love is saying to you, "It won't be long now. . . . Things are going to happen so fast your head will swim, one thing fast on the heels of the other. You won't be able to keep up. Everything will be happening at once—and everywhere you look, blessings!" (Amos 9:13-15, MSG, *The Message*).

> "And God is able to bless you abundantly, so that in all things at all times, having all that you need, you will abound in every good work."
>
> ———
>
> **2 CORINTHIANS 9:8, NIV**

You will find that the fruit of (y)our practice is very sweet and that you will have more than enough to enjoy and plenty to share. Joel Goldsmith, one of my favorite modern-day Christian mystics, would always say, "The vine consumeth not its own grapes." You will be given blessing upon blessing, and witness miracle upon miracle, in proportion to how much you Love, in proportion to how much you Forgive, and you will find that the Loving is the Forgiving.

The Promise is on the other side of forgiveness.

You're not seeing It yet because you haven't forgiven yet.

YOU MUST FORGIVE.

Yourself, others . . . for not recognizing that You, Yourself are the "others."

Loving is forgiving.

> "Meditate and become absorbed so that people will sense the 'ras' (Divine sweetness) in you, then you will have success."
>
> ————
>
> **ATTRIBUTED TO ANANDAMAYI MA**

.

PART ONE

Waking Up to Love

What's got you worried right now? Speak it into the Silence. That's how you surrender it.

That's how you give it to God—you give it to the Silence. And then you just keep hearing the Silence, you keep listening to the Silence. In the same way you were listening to the words of your worry, you listen to the Beauty of the Silence, and you become the Beautiful Silence.

And then worry becomes Prayer, and the mountain moves. That's Love.

"[Upon meeting with Love] even the beggar becomes a king, the lame persons are able to walk or even fly, the blind is able to see this universe, and many of the difficult writings of the destiny which are at the forehead of a person can be wiped out. Even the fundamental essence of a person or a personality or a being can be made to change."

MUKUNDA

"When you do Sadhana (spiritual practice) all lines on your hand change."

SRI SRI RAVI SHANKAR

"A moment with the beloved and the river changes its course."

RAM DASS

"To say that I am made in the image of God is to say that love is the reason for my existence, for God is love. Love is my true identity. Selflessness is my true self. Love is my true character. Love is my name."

THOMAS MERTON,
NEW SEEDS OF CONTEMPLATION

"Your outer journey may contain a million steps; your inner journey only has one: the step you are taking right now."

ECKHART TOLLE, *THE POWER OF NOW*

Before we begin, I'd like to share a practice that instantly points me to Love no matter where I am or what I'm doing. In a moment, close that body's eyes and see, in your mind's eye, the face of someone you love tremendously. See their smiling face. Or even their wagging tail and floppy ears! See them clearly and feel the Love you have for them. Feel the Love they have for you. And then turn from the mental image. Turn back to the darkness you see behind closed eyes, but don't turn away from the Love you're feeling. Keep smiling inside and outside. That mental image, that visualization, didn't cause the GoOD feeling, the Love you're experiencing now; it just pointed you to what was already here. As you open your eyes, don't stop feeling the Love. Don't let the appearance of the room, of the world that body is in, make you forget to feel the Love you are. **This Love is always here, always fresh. You just have to keep refreshing your attention.** Paying attention to Love is meditation.

Bowing into Love

THE QUOTE

"O Jesus, I surrender myself to you, take care of everything."

_____

FATHER DOLINDO RUOTOLO, *SURRENDER NOVENA*

THE PRACTICE

Bow, or Namaskar yourself into Love. Stay (t)here. And even as the body returns to its usual posture, continue to bow within, feel that humbled, loving Feeling inside, and bring it out into the world.

Whenever you feel overwhelmed, upset, angry, or fearful this week,
find a place where you can be alone,
and use your body like an antenna for the Divine.
Close your eyes, fold your hands in front of you,
and bow your head.
Feel the Silent-Peace that washes over you.
Hear how the thoughts quiet down.
Then bring that Love you found within out into the world.

Look out at the room you're in FROM the feeling of Love.
The room is appearing in the Love that you are.
The room IS Love.
If you aren't able to remove yourself and find somewhere private,
take this posture internally.
Feel into the Love inside that is (t)here,
no matter what that body is doing or not doing.

To bow or Namaskar is to bow from and as the Divinity, to the Divinity in and as the other. And although these days I appear to bow to everyone I meet, I'm actually only ever bowing to Love—the formless, invisible Presence I can feel where I see them. Everyone, every thing, every place is sacred, is "spiritualized," when you're aware of the Love that is everywhere. When Namaskar is practiced, you have baptized the moment, and everything that appears to be happening, with Love. This is how miracles are initiated.

"Everywhere I look I see only Ram [God/Love], and that's why
I'm always honoring everything."

—

NEEM KAROLI BABA,
QUOTED IN RAM DASS, *MIRACLE OF LOVE*

"All action is prayer. All trees are desire-fulfilling.
All water is the Ganga, all land is Varanasi. Love everything."

—

NEEM KAROLI BABA,
QUOTED IN RAM DASS, *MIRACLE OF LOVE*

I received a message from a *GoOD Mornings with CurlyNikki* listener named Julie. She wrote, "*Many say believe. Nikki, you say, be Love.*" And I was in the midst of making some plans for travel, very expensive plans for travel. And when I saw those words—which I don't remember saying, and I may have never said, but I definitely feel them and live them—it felt so good that I had to share them with you. Can you feel that? Do you resonate with that?

Believing in something is a heavier lift than being Love in this moment, being in Love, living as Love, feeling Love, being connected, plugged in consciously to this felt-faith. It's a completely different way to live, a completely different way to exist in this world. You go from surviving to actually thriving and flourishing and blossoming in This.

The practice of Namaskar, of bowing (internally and externally), will give you a way to move into feeling this Love in a very conscious way, in a very real way. There's a clip I once shared of Beyoncé from her HBO special where she was talking about this Love. She called it "a tingling," "a warmth." She said that she feels it when she looks at her children, when she looks at her husband. And she said, "It's God. It's Love. It's real." With tears in her eyes, she said, "I'm hot with it." And watching that video, I knew exactly what she was talking about. Her feeling It while speaking about It turned me toward It, and my eyes welled up, too. Meher Baba said that this Love is communicative. We pass it to each other, we catch it from each other. I'm a lit candle, and these words are a way of lighting your wick.

I used to notice spiritual teachers like Osho, Mooji, and Eckhart Tolle walking in the Namaskar posture—walking out onstage or among their followers with their hands clasped in prayer position in front of them. I always thought it was just a holy way to walk, just a holy way to look. But once you try it for yourself, you'll feel the power of it. It's like your folded hands keep you aware of the Love that's enfolding you. Holding your hands this way helps you hold the feeling of Love consciously. And to turn up the wattage, to increase the seeming power of this practice even more, lean forward and bow your head gently, too. Earlier in my practice, I would do this every day for fifteen minutes in my room, walking in a little circle with my eyes closed at times.

Do it now. Feel into It. Mooji says, "When you're in this posture, you can't have negative thoughts." Your body becomes an antenna for the Divine. You're using this position to feel into the silence of a positive mind, into your true state, into your GoOD feeling, your God state. And when you are in a situation where you can't Namaskar outwardly, take up this posture inside. Feel how it feels to bow physically on the outside and notice that you can experience the same Peace and Humbleness without moving the body an inch. The Love is here to feel and be, no matter how that body is being carried, but postures like this, especially in the beginning, make the Love more accessible.

So, however you're feeling right now, and I pray that you're feeling Love, see if you can take a screenshot of this Feeling inside, record It, feel It purely and vividly throughout your entire being, and then notice that you can pull It up anytime, anywhere! No matter how that body is feeling, no matter what or who it is seeing. Love is loving. You can paste this Feeling over everything. You can feel It in the middle of anything. You can hear It, Its Silence, in the midst of every thought.

If you have to go to the office today, or if you have to go to the grocery store tomorrow, or if you just get to chill today, run some errands, or go to the beach or play with the kids, whatever the case may be, you can take this experience, this pure feeling of Love, of divine Love, and paste it over every moment.

Driving down the road, this Love is louder than traffic. Walking to the kitchen, this Love is more real than dishes. It's just a simple shift in your attention from what you're seeing out here in the world to what you're feeling inside. Even if you're feeling upset, that's also on the outside. The upset is there, but this Love does not change. And you can use the Namaskar, the prayer hands, the bowing, to come back to yourself over and over again today, whether you do it physically with your hands or just internally, remembering the feeling that you find when you do that.

You don't have to do the prayer hands. You don't have to do anything to be yourself. You are Love always. Right now, you are that. And so these practices that I share with you are awesome permission slips. They're easy-access doors to get you back to remembering this, but you don't need them.

Whenever you find yourself in a moment that is overwhelming or just uncomfortable even in the slightest, come back to this. Do it. Take a moment. Go to the restroom, somewhere where you can be alone, and try the prayer hands to use that body as an antenna to come back to Love.

And then, with eyes closed, feeling Love clearly, open your eyes, lift your head, raise your chin, lower your hands to your sides, and bring that Love you found inside out into the world, out into your experience, out into the office, out into your home, and walk through that Love. Be that Love. Extend that Love. That's the work that we're doing. That's the only work there is.

I Love you.

> "God's Spirit of life approaches us so silently that we do not become aware of the presence immediately."
>
> ———
>
> **SAINT SOPHRONY (SAKHAROV)**
> **OF ESSEX**

Listening for the Feeling of Love

THE QUOTE

"Shift your attention from words to Silence and you will hear."

NISARGADATTA MAHARAJ, *I AM THAT*

THE PRACTICE

Every time you notice a negative thought, judgment, or criticism, notice the Silence that's right next to, behind, above, beneath, and pervading it. Simply notice the Silence the thought came from and dissolves back into. This turns the thought back into Love.

Today and every day this week, whenever you are met with a challenge in your external environment or even just challenging thoughts—

Close your eyes for a moment, and listen within.

Listen like you're listening for a sound you can't hear.

Thoughts may come,
but simply return to listening.
It will seem like nothing is happening,
but trust me.
Love is in that Silence.

Love is that Silence.
That Silence is Love,
and It's healing your thoughts (shifting them to the positive, as a
natural side effect)
and your world.
But you have to let It.
You have to surrender to this Silence, to this Love.
I call it listening for the feeling of Love.
Do this with me today, this week, and always.

"In every moment you only have one real choice: to be aware of
the Self or to identify with the body and the mind."

———————

ANNAMALAI SWAMI, *FINAL TALKS*

Almost immediately you'll begin to notice little winks from Love. I collect
them and encourage you to do the same. Keep a running note in your
phone called "Love Receipts" where you date and list the people, circumstances, conditions, thoughts, and moods that reinforced your
smile, this Love you're practicing. In moments of doubt or despair, just
scrolling back through your receipts will help you see that the more you
lean into what's beyond your thoughts and beyond your thinking, the
more your life flows. It'll help you stay true to this commitment of Silence over words.

A lot of people think that meditation is about silencing your thoughts
into submission. But this week you're learning that you don't have to wres-
tle your thoughts to the ground to achieve the Quiet. The Quiet is always,
already here, even in the midst of noise. If you're thinking, thinking, thinking, you'll have more thoughts that say you shouldn't be thinking, thinking,
thinking, and it complicates things and things get very messy very fast.

But if you can, notice what's right there with the thoughts: there's a Silence that's happening always, already, even when the thoughts are there and even when they're raging. Thoughts are going to do what they do. The mind is doing what it does, just like the breath is doing what it does, your stomach is doing what it does, your heart, thankfully, is doing what it does. Just like that, you just have to let your thoughts be, too.

The way you let those other processes be is to let your thoughts be. You don't try to change them. You don't have to acknowledge them and let them go. You just have to let them be and see what is right next to them. And so right now, you may hear yourself breathing, hear the ambient sounds around you, but can you hear the Silence that these sounds are coming from? Even if you can't hear the Silence yet (you will by the end of the week), in the "trying," the "turning," you are already successful. That is the practice.

The listening itself is the Silence, and the more you remember to just listen, the quieter you'll become inside.

"Real Silence means there is actually nowhere else
for the mind to go."

ANANDAMAYI MA, *WORDS OF SRI ANANDAMAYI MA*

Whenever you're met with a challenge in your external environment (which includes excessive thoughts), stop and close your eyes. If you're somewhere safe, you can do this right now. Just take a little pause, a little retreat, a little refresh, and listen within. Listen for the Silence. Listen like you're listening for a sound that you can't hear or like you're listening for a voice. Don't expect to hear a voice or words in your language (this Love existed before language). Just listen to nothing within.

Listen to the darkness you see behind closed eyes, like you're
waiting on it to tell you something.

Thoughts will come, but just return your attention to the listening, return your attention to the Silence. Take your attention off the words and put it back on to the Silence. It's just a muscle you're working. Your attention is a muscle. Right now, it might be weak and lazy, always resting in the words, in the thoughts. And so you're training it. This is the gym. And it feels like you're listening to nothing, like nothing is happening (just like the first few weeks at the actual gym!), but you're actually listening to God. Listening with Love, to Love. You're always hearing It, but now you know: God is in that Silence. God *is* that Silence. That Silence is Love.

That Silence is Love, and it's healing your thoughts. So you don't have to shift to positive thinking. When you are connected to, plugged in to, and consciously feeling this Love, your thoughts shift naturally to the positive. You have good thoughts, God thoughts, when you are plugged in consciously to your Source. A beautiful world is a natural side effect of you being connected to this inner Beauty, consciously.

I call it "listening for the feeling of Love." When I turn within right now as I appear to be writing these words, there's a loud Silence. There's a nothingness within. There are still thoughts; there's still the sound of these words pinging around in the Silence, still the sound of the keys being struck on the laptop, but it's all happening in the Silence. And in the awareness of Silence, this feeling of Love bubbles up and fills my entire being. In the beginning, it feels like I, Nikki, am feeling Love here in this body. And for a few years that was my truth: I felt like I was feeling Love. And as I continued to practice and work this muscle, it became very clear that this Love is not just here, it's not localized; it's everywhere. And so now, everywhere I look, I feel Love. I see the world, but I feel Love. If you were here in this room, where I could see you, I'd feel Love and know that as the truth and know that as your truth. And that's what oneness is.

Try This: *Put on some headphones or earbuds and play your favorite song—whatever song gets you feeling good, gets you feeling God—and don't listen to the music. Listen for the Silence that the music is coming from. Even if your headphones are on blast, which I do not recommend, you can become aware of Silence within, almost like a Silence within your head. Even though your ears are picking up this beautiful music that you Love so much, it's such a familiar song, there's a quiet that is loud. It's really loud. It's a quiet that is big, bigger than the notes, bigger than the moment when they drop the beat or change the tempo or rhythm (my favorite part of every song!). You just have to listen for it and know how to turn to it. And once you recognize it, you could be at a rock concert, you could be at the beach with a bunch of families and kids yelling and the waves crashing, and there It is.*

If you can, just hold on to that Silence like it's a thread, hold on to it like a thread through every moment that you find that body in. Every moment, like right now, you're listening to this or maybe you're seated at home reading these words, maybe you're in the car, that's this moment. No matter what scene you find that body in; it changes all day. You're holding that thread. You're staying aware of that Silence that's behind the noisiness, behind the loud, drama-full scenes.

*That's what we're doing. It's very, very easy to do. You just have to **remember to remember** to practice, and that's why you have Me. This is a good morning. It's a God morning, and you're remembering who you are. You're remembering the Silence, and you're remembering that all of your abundance and all of your Love, your healthy relationships, your health, everything, your purpose, unfolds from this Silent-Love.*

I Love you.

Focusing on Love

THE QUOTE

"There's really only one problem, distraction.
And therefore, only one solution, mindfulness."

DZONGSAR KHYENTSE RINPOCHE, J. C. AMBERCHELE,
COMING TO NOTHING AND FINDING EVERYTHING

THE PRACTICE

Every time something comes into your awareness—a thought, emotion, person, or circumstance—think (hear inside) "Distraction," and notice the Love you were distracted from. Look at the Love. Focus on Love again.

A mind full of God,
a heart full of love.
How is your heart today?
Listen until it fills up again.
Listen like God is going to tell you the secret.
*But **this** is the secret.*
If you could just invite this in when you're feeling overwhelmed today,

or too busy to rest, to stop.
When you're feeling like you don't know what to do,
this becomes your next step.
Every time something comes into your awareness—
a thought,
an emotion,
a person—
think "Distraction"
and turn back to This.
Come back to This.
Love this.

Saint Seraphim of Sarov called it "the acquisition of the Holy Spirit," which he said is the sole purpose of Christianity. In a conversation between Saint Seraphim and a Christian named Nicholas Motovilov in the middle of a cold and snowy forest in Russia in the early 1800s, the latter asked the saint, "How can I discern for myself [the Spirit of God's] true manifestation in me?" Saint Seraphim took Motovilov firmly by the shoulder and said, "We are both in the Spirit of God right now, my son. Why don't you look at me?" Motovilov replied, "I cannot look, Father, because your eyes are flashing like lightning. Your face has become brighter than the sun, and my eyes ache with pain."

"And Saint Seraphim said, "Don't be alarmed, your Godliness! Now
you yourself have become as bright as I am. You are now in the
fullness of the Spirit of God yourself; otherwise you would not be
able to see me as I am."

SAINT SERAPHIM OF SAROV,
ON THE ACQUISITION OF THE HOLY SPIRIT

You are now in the fullness of the Spirit of God.

Mind full, heart full, soul full.

"If riches increase, set not your heart on them" (Psalm 62:10, AMPC).

When opportunities come, when all the doors are thrown open because of how you've opened yourself to grace, set not your heart on them.

Keep your heart here, in this.

Remembering that God is your provider, not what He has turned into, not what He has seemed to become. The riches don't provide, the opportunities don't provide. They appear because of Him, because of This. That you're hearing and feeling in abundance. It's always Here. And when you live out from It, you always have.

But the mind will whisper that you don't.

Like a snake, it will hiss and tell you what you need to make you happy.

Dr. Morgan Francis said, "My most frequent complaint toward my partner or loved one reveals my greatest emotional need, not their greatest flaw."

Say that to yourself, with your partner in mind or with your boss in mind. "My most frequent complaint toward them reveals my greatest emotional need, not their greatest flaw."

It reveals your mind,
your ego,
your seeming separation from God,
your forgetfulness of This.
Because if you had This,
if you remembered This,
if you were hearing This,
feeling This,
you wouldn't need anything.
When you turn away from This,
you need compliments.
You need validation.

You need security.
You need Love.
You're needing what you already have,
what You already are,
like a wave looking for water,
a sunbeam looking for light.
You're already That.
This Fullness is your purpose.
Being full of Silence,
feeling full of Love.
Pour yourself into your Self right now.
Feel It starting at your toes,
and going up your legs,
and up through your belly and your chest,
down your arms,
into your head.
And hold It.
Keep holding It.
Don't be distracted by that thought that hisses, "What if I can't hold It later?"
Later won't come when you're here;
when you are aware of This,
there is no later.
You just have to hold It now.
Ram Dass said, "Ask yourself: Where am I?
Answer: Here.
Ask yourself: What time is it?
Answer: Now.
Say it until you can hear it."
Until you can hear this Silence.
Until you can hear God's Name,
the one that is so hallowed,

so holy,
that you can't speak It.
All you can do is hear It,
hear Him announcing His presence where you are,
His fullness where you are.
They can't touch you where You are.

> "Forgive them. All of your thems. The more thems you can forgive,
> the lighter you'll feel."
>
> ———————
>
> MIKE FOSTER (@MIKEFOSTER2000 ON INSTAGRAM)

Include yourself in "them," for thinking you weren't worthy of
this Love,
for keeping yourself from feeling this Love,
for keeping yourself distracted, believing in a "them."
A Persian proverb says, "Take your attention off the forms,
and focus on what's inside."
Turn to this Love and say,
"Lead me to the rock that is higher than I" (Psalm 61:2),
and then don't come back down.
Not for anything.
You help from up here,
from (t)His Altitude,
from this Vibration,
from this Love;
not from anger,
not from pity or frustration.
You help from Love,
and you pull everybody up with you.

Your mind is agitated because you keep trying to still it.
That is not what I have called you to do.
I called you to hear what is also here—
To hear My Silence even as your thoughts race.
To listen for My Still, Small Voice in the tumult of your day.
My Stillness stills you.
There is no other way.
Today I want you to look right at what's disturbing you,
whether that's in the mirror, or in your inbox, your account,
or on your couch or behind that desk at your office,
and this time, don't listen to yourself,
those familiar judgments and criticisms;
listen to Me.
But I won't use words.
I Am that Stream of Silence,
that quiet, loving Feeling that allows you to trust that the world
is new,
even though it appears unchanged.
My Loving Silence is the first and the last Sign.
Live in My Whisper,
And It will be done.

I used to think that quieting the mind was my job. I was afraid of my mind—the Law of Attraction, popularized by the book *The Secret* in 2006, taught me that good thoughts made good things happen and bad thoughts brought about bad things. That the life you are living is a direct result of your thoughts. But the eastern teachings I later found would ask, "If the voice in your head is you, then who is listening to it?" Once I became aware of and AS this Awareness, everything changed for the better, especially my formal meditations. The more I sat down on the mat, the more I saw that no matter what, after about twenty minutes, the mind would naturally quiet down. It would settle because the body was settled, the breath was settled. And then the attention that was flitting here and there settled in, on, and AS the Stillness I had been so desperately looking and working for. This Stillness or Love is always here. You don't have to become Still; you just have to wake up AS that place that is Still, that is God, that is beyond the concepts of good, healed, and wealth, that is Everything. In the Bible, we are told, "Seek ye first the Kingdom, and all else will be added." Turn toward the Kingdom of Love inside, and all your good, health, and abundance will be added. Today, find a quiet place where you won't be disturbed, and when you have no pressing appointments scheduled right after, set an alarm for thirty minutes and sit or lie down (if you fall asleep, wake up and set it again!). Decide that you won't get up until that alarm goes off! And then notice what's noticing "you."

"Your awareness of this invisible God field gets interpreted through your human brain as your Good, in every way."

HERB FITCH

Relaxing into Love

THE QUOTE

"The light has come. You are healed and you can heal. The light has come. You are saved and you can save. You are at peace, and you bring peace with you wherever you go. Darkness and turmoil and death have disappeared. The light has come.

"Today we celebrate the happy ending to your long dream of disaster. There are no dark dreams now. The light has come. Today the time of light begins for you and everyone. It is a new era, in which a new world is born. The old one has left no trace upon it in its passing. Today we see a different world, because the light has come."

———————

A COURSE IN MIRACLES

THE PRACTICE

Become aware of your body. Feel how your giving it attention relaxes it automatically. Notice the Lightness that was always here. Be the Light.

"How am I?"

That's a question I want you asking multiple times a day this week.

Check in. And you can use your attention like a scanner and just run through your body and see if it's trying to tell you something.

We hold so much tension in our body, in our shoulders.
Relax them right now.
See if you can relax your shoulders more. Try to relax your stomach more.
Relax your toes. Relax your jaw, your face.
Notice that you're breathing. Feel Love for your breathing. Be grateful for that process.
We have to check in with ourselves during the day. These little checkups, they're essential.
Our ego is like our armor, and we put it on and then we forget it's on, and then we wonder why we're so tired.
Every day, at the end of the day,
we're exhausted because we're carrying around this tension, this heaviness.
Ego is tension.
Spirit, Soul, this I Am—Love is what you are, and it feels more like relaxation.
It feels more like the way you feel right now.
Softened. Lighter. You've become the Light Itself.

We don't have to make this Light something vague and mystical. We can just make it about awareness. Awareness is this Light. Awareness of your body relaxing. You can even set your phone to go off every hour on the hour. Just set a little alarm, and on that alarm, as you're turning it off, scan your body; it takes less than a second to do. Use your attention, your awareness, to scan the body, and notice that the relaxation takes place automatically. You don't have to try to relax or to try to let go; the "letting go" is the natural result of Awareness. When you're aware, you're relaxed. When you're aware, you're Love. After much practice,

Ram Dass arrived at his final teaching, "I Am Loving Awareness." In Pure Awareness there are no bodies to be tense, no egos to transcend. There's just Love-Light.

> "Establish peace within yourself. Healing is not difficult when we know that we are not trying to heal a body, improve or change man. We are only trying to establish in our consciousness the awareness of the peace that is already there. Do not seek healing, seek peace; the healing is the added thing."
>
> ———————
>
> **GIL MICHAELS**

And the more you are aware of that lightness of being inside that body you appear to be, the more you begin to see that Lightness of being outside of you, in the people you meet and in your circumstances. Your awareness inside dissolves tension. That same awareness outside dissolves problems. Lightness inside, Light outside. Love everywhere.

This Awareness sounds like Silence and feels like Love. In a short while, you'll see It's Light, too, at first as flashes or pulses behind closed eyes while in formal meditation, sometimes in your peripheral vision as you go about your day, but you'll shortly discern that you're not just seeing Light; you are the Light. And because you know yourself as That, you know the others as That, too. That's real Love. Knowing there are no others—only Light is here. Only Love is real.
This Real Light is not the opposite of darkness. It sees/knows the worldly light and the darkness. It's what you see the darkness behind closed eyes with.

"Are you going to swim?" my seatmate on the tour bus, Sandra, asked me. We were riding through northern Israel with a small group. Although Sandra and I had never met before, she felt like family. She knew things about me she shouldn't have and invited me to revisit my beliefs about intimate relationships and how they could fit into a very spiritual life. She also invited me to swim with her in the River Jordan. I was staying at a pilgrimage center at the Church of the Multiplication on the Sea of Galilee. I had gotten my toes wet and blessed myself there, and I assumed I'd do the same at the famed and holy River Jordan. I didn't even have a swimsuit.

Sandra and I shared our spiritual journeys as the bus wove through biblical town after biblical town, like Capernaum and Cana. We stopped to tour places like Jesus's childhood home and the first place He taught publicly. And finally, on our last stretch together, just fifteen minutes before our arrival at the River Jordan, Sandra said, "I want to be baptized again. I will be baptized at the River Jordan—I heard it's possible." And it was as if a light came on inside me. Those words lit a fire in me. I "wanted" to be baptized again, too, and what better place than where Jesus was baptized by John the Baptist?! It was done. Even though we arrived fifteen minutes after the site's closing. Even though we were told we couldn't be supplied with baptismal robes and that were no baptists on-site, that we would've had to bring one with us. I stood there listening to our tour guide speaking with the strict staff. And while these ears could hear what was being said, I could hear what He was saying. I knew I was stepping into a moment already in progress. There was some anxiety present, some ego there, but there was a deeper calm, a stillness, a surety. A Light.

And then the "hereness" appeared as me in a stall changing into a white robe with nothing but my underwear underneath (I'd later learn that said robe turns sheer when wet!). It then appeared as this body standing before a bathroom mirror, removing its turban and securing belongings. Next, the Now rearranged and appeared as this body walking toward the River Jordan. As I got closer, I could see a small line of people and two men in the water. There were still baptists on-site! But they were a private group from a church in Georgia. I walked right up to a woman who looked like a leader of the group and asked if they had time for three more—myself, Sandra, and Joyce, another new friend from the tour group. The woman was the first lady, the wife of one of the pastors in the water. She asked him and he looked at me, looked back at her, smiled, and shrugged his shoulders as to say, "Why not?" I stepped down into the water; it was absolutely frigid but clear, clean. So cold, though. In any other situation, I would've never just walked in. I would have taken a while to acclimate, to adjust, to likely chicken out and sit pretty by the shore. But I walked out on faith, and the two pastors, Jim and James, greeted me and asked about my path and shared about theirs. The water was so cold and my muscles were so tense. And that tensing, because of years of practice, triggered my practice. A softening occurred right there in the water. The resistance was gone. The noisy mind was gone. "Me" was gone. Only "I" was. Then the moment appeared as total submersion, without enough time even to hold my nose. I could see the Light dancing on the water's surface above me. I was submerged in water but being baptized by Light, by the Fire that was lit in me on that tour bus. Being baptized wasn't "my" desire. It was My Destiny. The eyes closed to savor the Sweetness, and then there was hugging, and thanking. Loving.

"John said, 'I indeed baptize you with water unto repentance, but He who is coming after me is mightier than I, whose sandals I am not worthy to carry. He will baptize you with the Holy Spirit and fire.'"

MATTHEW 3:11, NKJV

Praying (Ceaselessly) into Love

THE QUOTE

"When prayer becomes habit, miracles become your lifestyle."

———————

UNKNOWN

Prayer is defined here not as words but as the awareness of Love, the union with Love, with the One Presence.

THE PRACTICE

Feel Peace inside, hear Silence inside. That's true Prayer.
Feel Love within and know It as your true Self.
Know It as the Self of everyone and everything.
There is only this Peace, this Love.
And when you're in touch with That,
conscious of It,
miracles become commonplace.

Relax and know that the felt-Presence of God, of Love, is true prayer.

Fun fact: I used to keep an AirPod in one ear—sometimes it would be playing spiritual music, sometimes a spiritual talk, but at all times it was as if I had one ear in the Kingdom as I moved about in the world. It would help me keep my attention on Truth while I was seeing the false, the impermanence, the appearances that Jesus told us not to judge by. So I'd keep one foot in the Kingdom to remind me that I am actually in Heaven, that heaven is not a place, that it is a state of being, an inner contentment, an inner "hush." And that's what we're practicing this week.

Herb Fitch, a teacher of Joel Goldsmith's Infinite Way, told a story about a little boy who had been hungry for a couple of days while his father was away. Then his father showed up at home and opened the door, his arms full of food—bread and cheese and milk, snacks like cakes, cookies, and pies. And Herb asked, "Do you think that the boy would then fall to his knees and pray and say, 'Father, feed me, father,' or that he would be shouting or crying out, 'Father, I need some food. Give me some food, please,' or, would he quietly assume, now that his father is there, that his hunger is at an end?" In the presence of his father, not a word need be spoken. He would trust that his father knew his needs and was there to provide for him.

But that's not how we pray. Even if we are already beyond seeing God as a person, like a human figure that is giving or withholding stuff, even if we're seeing God now or feeling God as a presence, a formless presence, we still think we need words, that we need to consult and explain to God what is needed. Even though we might say we know that God is all-knowing, we say, "Well, we've got to inform. We need to consult and let Him know what is needed here."

True prayer is not a prayer of words or supplication. It's just becoming aware of this Presence and knowing this Loving Presence as God as your deepest self, and staying aware of it. That communion, that Union, is prayer. And once you're in contact with It, It becomes the needed things. It becomes the added things. It becomes the outer forms that you require for a full life. God fulfills Itself through and AS you.

Someone asked Mother Teresa how she prays and her response was that she just listens to God. When asked what God says, she replied that

He doesn't do anything either, He just listens! She's listening. God's listening. What does that sound like? Silence. A Love-filled Silence that she was and is paying attention to. A Silence that she (and you) has always existed as.

> "The Lord hears us more readily than we suspect;
> it is our listening to Him that needs to be improved."
>
> ———————
>
> BISHOP FULTON SHEEN, *GO TO HEAVEN*

This week, you'll stay in this Silence and let your miracles unfold from (t)here. That's where the miracles come from: from the Silence. The Silence is the miracle, but it unfolds as the outer miracle. The things that you're waiting for right now, the things that you're wanting, that you've been wanting for years, that you've been looking for, they will come when you get in the Quiet, when you start resting there, when you start knowing yourself as That, and when you start giving It time.

> "When I am with you, everything is prayer, everything."
>
> ———————
>
> ATTRIBUTED TO RUMI

Practice communing with God until you recognize that there is no need for communion or union because you were never separate. There's only One, and you are That. But until then, we practice—knowing in this moment that we are now together, seemingly two. You hear or see my words, you're aware of yourself there, feeling our Oneness, this Peace that you feel when you're with me here; this Peace is the Peace of my being. It's the Peace of your being, of your neighbor's being, of your mother's being, whether your mother is here physically or not. My grandmother left this Earth physically in 2015, but her being, this being, still is. It doesn't go anywhere. It doesn't change.

And so all during the day, each day this week, practice remembering, knowing, and feeling the Oneness. Not believing in Oneness or imagining Oneness. Experiencing It in every moment, "good" and "bad." So that no moment makes you forget this. Not even the scary ones. Even in the scariest moments, you get to be triggered back into remembering this Truth, that there's only one Power, one Being, one Love. Shout-out to Bob Marley. He got it. He knew this, lived this.

I Love you.

Catching the Love Train (How Grace Works)

Keep forgiving yourself for judging by appearances. Keep forgiving yourself for believing in this world. You forgive the instant you remember God . . . the moment you pause and feel for the Silent-Love. Forgiveness is allowing the Love you are to flow into the scene . . . into the world appearance. Feeling Love while moving through the world disappears problems. Love is the solution you've been looking for. It is the miracle. And It is you. Which means It's here, now. Smile. When you're on the Love Train, forgiveness comes naturally. You see there's no one to forgive and no one to do the forgiving. Loving is forgiving. It's surrendering. It's letting go and letting God be the conductor.

THE QUOTES

"When you run alone it's called a race, but when God runs with you, It's called Grace,"

UNKNOWN

"It's like this whole life we've been running, running, running hard. We're exhausted, we're tired, sweaty. And then we look to the left and we notice there's a train right there next to us running too, and that all we've had to do this whole time is just get on the train. The train's running in the same direction that we are, and it can carry us."

————————

HERB FITCH

THE PRACTICE

Recognize that all this life, you've been running, hard, right next to a train that's running in the same direction. Get on it. Sit down. REST. RELAX. Take a load off. Breathe. Smile. You're being carried. Feel Love for this realization. Don't get off this train. Repeat the mantra, "I am on the train."

So, we see the train and we hop on it.

Sit down and catch your breath and rest, abide, Love, relax your shoulders, relax your stomach, relax your thighs and your feet, your toes, your jaw.

Let everything melt. Melt into whatever you're sitting on.
Place your right hand over your heart,
close your eyes and feel Love for your breath.
Feel gratitude for your breathing.
Feel Love for your heart beating.
You can even feel Love for those thoughts that are running through.
Feel Love for those thoughts.
You don't have to think about the thoughts.
You don't have to judge them.
You can Love them.
Love the thoughts.
Love the breath.
Love your heart beating.
Love this feeling of Love.
Love the relaxation you're in now.

Love the idea that you've been running so hard that you forgot to notice the train running right next to you.

Love that you're now seated on that train.

You know that feeling when you finally sit down in that seat on that flight you thought you were going to miss? The one you had to drop your cool for and actually make a mad dash through the airport for? Recall that sense of relief. That moment when you looked up at the air vent above your head and silently thanked God. The coolness you felt returning after the sweat, the heat you worked up. That. That feeling, that deep exhale, all the time.

Everything will be easier now, going forward. Effortless flow.
You are being carried.
You've always been carried,
but now you know you can feel it,
you are consciously aware of the flow of
this Love where you are.
And you are in tune with It.
You are in alignment with It.
You let It use you.
You let It speak through you.
It always knows the right thing to say.
It always knows what to do in any situation.
All you have to do is stay aware that you are one with It,
that It is you,
but you don't have to pray to It with words or beg It to do this or that.
You don't have to direct It or send It out.
You just sit in this, and know everything is This.
There's nothing that you come into contact with during the day that is not This.
And what does that mean?

There's nothing to fear.
There's no one to fear.
It's all You.
There's just this Presence right now appearing as these words.
Later, it might appear as your boss,
but if you can remember, when you are registering that moment
with that familiar face of your boss,
if you can just pause,
take a pause while you're listening to what they're saying to you
and see through them to the reality,
through the conditioning,
through the concepts,
through the history,
in that moment,
history has ended.
There's no concept of that seeming person.
There is no person there.
There's just the Christ,
just Love,
just God,
just This.
And then you'll notice the body talking back to the boss, saying
whatever's appropriate for that moment.
And the boss will say some other words.
And that moment will be over.
And then there'll be the next moment.
And it'll be up to you again to recognize that there are not people here.
There is just Love here appearing as people,
people who you can Love,
maybe not their form, their humanity—sometimes it's difficult, it's
challenging—but this God Love that is here,
that is truly here.

It can't help but to Love.
Just like the sun is shining,
this Love is loving.
And when you're abiding in and as That,
That's all you can do, too.
That's all you can do.

And so this week, you can have a little mantra, just a little triggering re-membrance: "I'm on the train." This is effortless flow. Love is carrying me. Everything is this Love. There is nothing that is not this Love. Love moving through Love.

Effortless.

"Christ with me,
Christ before me,
Christ behind me,
Christ in me,
Christ beneath me,
Christ above me,
Christ on my right, Christ on my left,
Christ when I lie down, Christ when I sit down,
Christ when I arise,
Christ in the heart of every one who thinks of me,
Christ in the mouth of everyone who speaks of me,
Christ in every eye that sees me,
Christ in every ear that hears me."

SAINT PATRICK

Smelling Love's Hidden Perfume

Remembering God is our main business, and that remembrance handles all of our other business! So all of the senses must be employed toward that end.

THE QUOTE

"You contain within your innermost being many qualities of which you are unaware. These are like unto beautiful bottles of rare perfume which you have put away in closets and forgotten."

———————

EVA BELL WERBER, *THE JOURNEY WITH THE MASTER*

THE PRACTICE

Allow a fragrant oil (I like Jasmine Absolute in Jojoba Oil from Whole Foods) to jog your memory to reach for God, to stay tapped into Love. Or light a stick of incense to help you stay aware of the Light in your heart. Let the worldly perfume guide you to your inner, hidden "rare perfume," in the words of Eva Bell Werber. Do what it takes to BE who you are.

Relax your shoulders,

relax your stomach

and your face.

Breathe in Love,

breathe out Love.

Each breath in, Love.

Feel the gentle Sweetness inside your chest.

Let each breath take you into your heart, and as you breathe in

Love and breathe out Love,

feel that space soften.

Feel it melt.

Feel it getting warmer.

Feel the gentle vibration there.

Right where you're sitting,

right where you are,

right now,

God is.

You are home in God,

in Love.

And that means you are safe.

You are truly secure,

you are Loved,

and this Love has always been here.

It's not that It comes closer to you in moments like this;

It's just that you've turned toward It.
If you could stay here,
even for just twenty-four hours,
the changes you would notice seemingly within and without would
motivate you to stay turned toward God,
to stay turned to Love.

You turn to love until no one's left to do the turning.

I found my bottle of jasmine oil. I had hidden it from myself, trying to hide it from my kids, because they love it. And when I became aware of the smell, it jogged my memory to turn to Love, to return to God, because it's not something I smell regularly. It's the reason why a lot of people burn incense. It's just another way to keep you in the presence of God, to keep reminding you that God is where you are. You can collect and hang human renderings of God, you can place sticky notes everywhere to remind you to feel God, but the sense of smell is a powerful trigger, too!

For a while, I had an icon of Jesus and one of Maharajji sitting near my bedside. One day, I did a bit of spring cleaning and rearranged my room. I remember sitting down on my bed a few days later, noticing thoughts, and looked to the icons for Presence. They weren't there, but the Love still was. I smiled at the empty space where the icons used to be. Which came first, the thought to look in the direction of the icons or the feeling of Love? As you wake up more and more to Love, ask yourself that question. Did you remember to practice in this moment, or was the practice already happening and you woke up to seeing that it was? The mind is always taking credit for what God is already doing through you.

When I was sitting at my little altar last night, doing my practice with jasmine on my wrists for the first time in a long time, every time that smell hit me, it pointed me back to that inner perfume, the inner sweetness, the feel of the Divine. Just as I listen for the Feeling of Love, I can smell for the Feeling of Love. I can look through the appearances to the Feeling of Love. Every sense can carry you back to This.

> "All sensory pleasures in the world are like a wrapping paper; the true bliss is the presence inside."
>
> **SRI SRI RAVI SHANKAR**

And so the practice this week is to keep remembering this Hidden Perfume and to use some form of an outer perfume to guide you back to that remembrance. That outer fragrance could be an incense stick. If you have one, burn it, and as you're burning it, intend to remember God for the whole time it's lit. Keep the flame in your heart lit while that incense is lit. Or you can dab on a little bit of essential oil (mixed with and diluted by a carrier oil for safety). There are a million different fragrances. Pick one you don't usually smell (so it won't just fade to the background). Pick the one that most resonates with you, dab some on, and every time you catch that whiff, feel Love. Allow the worldly fragrance to remind you of your Godly Fragrance, and you become more aligned, more open, more receptive, more attuned. You become the Fragrance. You recognize that you are the Fragrance, and because of that, you appear as an image of that Fragrance, as an image of Love.

Bonus: Begin to notice when your olfactory memory is triggered. In times of Peace, even in times of turbulence, I'll catch a faint hint of my Grandma Maxine's perfume. Many times, I've smelled phantom jasmine so strongly that I asked the people with me if they could smell it, too. Grace descends as beautiful fragrances to point you toward and beyond that which is smelling. Beyond that which is aware of the remembering. That which is excited about the "sign" of a GoOD smell coming from seemingly nowhere. Everything, every smell, points back to your refuge, brings you back Home.

"As the heavenly water begins to surge from the spring deep inside us, it spreads and expands our whole inner being and gives rise to ineffable blessings. The soul herself cannot even understand what is unfolding here. She senses a certain fragrance, we could say, as if within the depths of her being there were burning coals sprinkled with sweet perfumes. We cannot see the light or locate the source of the fire, but the sweet-smelling warmth permeates the whole of the soul and maybe even spreads into the body.

"Look. Try to understand what I'm saying. We don't actually feel heat or smell an aroma. The experience is far more delicate than that. Even if you have not gone through these things yourself, you must know that they really do happen. The soul perceives and understands this more clearly than my mere words could ever express. No matter how intensely we may crave spiritual delight, we cannot acquire it through our own efforts. It is not forged of the same metal that we are but is made from the purest gold of divine wisdom."

———————

SAINT TERESA OF AVILA, *THE INTERIOR CASTLE*

Affirming Love (The Quickest Way)

Feel Love inside. Know It as your Self. Stay (t)here.

THE QUOTES

"There is no other God than this sense of presence. And I Am this sense of presence. Understanding this with conviction is the quickest way."

―――――――――

ATTRIBUTED TO NISARGADATTA MAHARAJ

"Going within isn't a direction, it's a dimension."

―――――――――

SADHGURU

THE PRACTICE

Return to this mantra repeatedly, today: "I Am this Presence."
There is only Presence here.
You aren't becoming aware of the "Now,"
because you ARE the now.

You aren't becoming aware of Presence.
You ARE Presence.
You aren't becoming aware of Love.
You ARE Love.
And this can be your lived experience,
with eyes open during the day.
But you have to practice it every morning for the rest of your life.
But let's start with this week.
For a moment, close your eyes
and just become aware of your breathing,
appreciating your breath,
knowing that every breath is a gift from God,
from Love.
Feel Love for your breath.
Feel Love for every breath.
Allow that face to smile just a little.
As you continue to feel Love for your breathing,
become aware of this presence that's here.
It might feel like a vibration or a tingling, a warmth or a little joy
inside.
Become aware of this dimension of Presence that is right here,
right now.
It sounds like the Silence that these words are coming in and out of.
The Silence you can hear as the little voice inside repeats the words
that these fingers are tapping out.
And your body seems to sense this Silence as Love.
Your body is now just this Love.
Only this Love is here and it's boundless and it's invisible.
This is the body of Christ.

> "Love itself is the actual form of God."
>
> ———
>
> **SRI RAMANA MAHARSHI**

Love is your transcendental body. Your eternal body.

It can't be seen,
but you can be It because you are It.
In the Bible, Jesus says, "I and My Father are one."
That's another way of saying, 'I am this Presence."

For a while in the beginning, it'll feel like it's you AND this Presence. You becoming aware of Love. Right now it may feel that way to you, you aware of a Love that Nikki is pointing to. But there are not two where you are. There are not two anywhere.

There's just this Presence. There's not "God and you," in Joel Goldsmith's words, or the Presence and you. In this moment, consciously, you know there's just the Presence. There's just Love. You have to practice this felt-knowing when you have time alone because the world is loud and alluring. It's shiny, attention-getting, but you have to be able to walk through it as if you're blind.

So this week's practice is the mantra, "I am this presence." We are taking the duality out of it, not I am aware of this presence. And so you're just taking out the two. You're dissolving into the Presence. You're allowing the Presence to replace you and the world entirely. It's just Presence. I am. I am this Presence. Period. And allow that thought to come up today. Write it on your hand. I like to write things along my thumb, on the outside of my thumb so I can see it much of the day. You can put it on your screensaver. Make a sticky note. Put it on your computer screen, on your laptop, just to keep revisiting that.

"I am this Presence." When you know this, when it moves from belief and hoping that it is the case to the felt-recognition of it being so, that's when the signs follow.

The signs don't come first; they follow.
And so let's live in this mantra.
Let's live this mantra every day this week;
You are the Mantra.
I love you.

Say the mantra internally when the mind is quiet, but say it externally—out loud—when the mind is loud. And simply hear the sound of the words. Hear the words you are pronouncing, feel the tongue moving, feel the Love the words are pointing to. Where did the rogue thoughts go? Exactly. They are nothing, returned to Nothing. Forms of Love returned to the Big Love. Little waves in the Ocean of Love.

While in Galilee, Israel, I was on the phone with my sister, Syl, catching her up on what I'm up to and checking in on Gia and Max, when these two beautiful Sisters approached me asking me if I'm a Sister. At first I thought they were asking if I was speaking to my sister, so I was confused, but I caught on quickly when they asked "what Order are you from?" Syl, overhearing the conversation was totally amused and told me to tell them my name was Sister Mary Clarence (Sister Act). I did not! I told them that with my present lifestyle, I feel like a nun, and Sister Grazielle told me that I Am. I jokingly gestured as if I was following them back to the convent to sign up, and we laughed and shared until Sister Grazielle stopped, and with a serious face pointed at me, and then pointed at her ear and instructed, "keep listening to Him." She told me that she's praying for me. That sat on my Heart all night. After Mass that morning, I approached her and requested a one-on-one and she obliged! How Divine—to be able to speak with someone whose vocation it is to Listen . . . to Love. I'm in Love!

I Am Love!

"You've been Listening. I can tell. I know." She said as we sat down in an empty chapel to talk. She said it was my "aura and openness" that got her attention that week, seeing me at the church and around the grounds. I immediately launched into the questions I had typed out in my phone notes and she gently interrupted me by putting up one hand. And then she put both hands up and began praying for the Holy Spirit to descend and to speak through us and to bless all who would hear our interchange.

After briefly explaining what I do and how I can't become a nun because I have young children, she said, "You and I are the same, in different situations. The Holy Spirit does your work. You just Listen. He does my work. I just Listen. We can't forget that. When we die, St. Peter will ask us all the same one question—', how much did you Love?' whether you're a doctor, a bishop, a nun, or a podcaster . . .' how much did you Love?'

"God has no eyes, no arms, so He uses us. He uses our hands. He uses our mouths like Isaiah. He puts words into your mouth if you Listen."

On Experiencing the Presence

I asked her if she hears words or feels a feeling (like I do), and she said that she "hears in the ear of her Heart . . . we put ourselves into His Presence, that's how we Listen . . . a contemplative attitude all the time."

Every time she touched my shoulder or my forearm as she explained, BLISS. Calm, gentle, waves of Bliss. Her words flowed effortlessly, her presence was His.

On Work

She said to see every job as "the Lord is calling me!" She smiled big. "When I see trash on the ground and I'm in a hurry, I slow down and stop to pick it up saying, 'the Lord is calling me!' When you have Love of the Lord you can make a sacrifice, you can do all work, no matter what it is, with Love for Him. Just always be aware of him in every work and pray before you start anything!" I tried to launch into my litany of questions when we first sat down, and she stopped me and looked away, eyes closed, and said, "first, we pray."

On Love

She said if you Love God with the same flavor of Love you feel for a boyfriend or girlfriend, you will Love everyone automatically. If you Love God, you Love His children. "When we love God, it's not just for Him, it's for everyone."

On Suffering

I told her I had always been hesitant to take up my cross and follow Jesus because of all of the tragic stories of suffering I've read from the saints and other holy people. I asked how to get past this fear. She smiled knowingly and said, "We need it. It's a purification for us. When you suffer, it's like you empty yourself and you can feel that you are taking on some of the suffering of the world as a service . . . sharing in Jesus' suffering as a small sacrifice. Just offer your suffering to Him. Also when you have a grateful heart, know that it won't feel like suffering."

On Discerning His Will versus Our Will

I asked her how to tell our will from His, and she said, "you can answer that. We all can. When we do our own will it is limited. We can't help but make mistakes. Our Love becomes deformed. You want praise and other people to praise you. When it's His will, you don't have any 'want.'

You don't need praises, you don't need recognition, it's natural. Like giving gifts from the heart, you don't need or want anything in return. When you give gifts with love it's different. When you live from His Will, it's different. You can feel it. When I make decisions I ask the Lord, 'is this your will?' And listen. Then I do everything I can and at the end I say, 'Lord I did my best and I know you will do the rest.' And he does. Every time. Tell God, 'I trust you . . . no machine can destroy what you Will for me.' And when you succeed, don't act surprised! Know He did it!"

Repetition and Prayer

I asked her about praying the Rosary. She said she uses it to attune herself. And as she's speaking her eyes are closed and she's moving her hands in a flowing circular motion in front of her body and she's rocking gently (like we do!). She said saying the same prayer over and over, "you become a part of the prayer . . . when you're praying, your mind is with the prayer only and you put yourself into it. It's not how many times. It's attunement. The Rosary is the companion of the gospel. It contains the whole mystery of Jesus."

The Name

I asked her about which name of Jesus she most loves (Yeshua, Easho, Yesu, Ieso, etc) and she said, "We are only for, and of one God. No need of explaining or trying to figure it out. We have a deep connection. We are all calling the same One whether we know it or not (no matter the religion). We are all sons of Abraham."

When I asked her about when she heard The Call, she said she was 12, Up until then she wanted to be a soldier! She said the Lord changed it at 12 years old. " If you name what is in your heart you can take the action and it will happen. Pray. When in doubt pray. Ask the Holy Spirit. He will stir your heart and you will know what to do."

She told me to tell you that she loves you.

You are Love. And I Am, too.

Look Over Thoughts' Shoulder at Love

THE QUOTE

"Your thoughts will be okay without you. Rest."

————————

JAIYA JOHN

THE PRACTICE

Sit formally for 5–10 minutes and as thoughts come, look over their shoulder.
Sit in a quiet place and look past and beyond each thought that appears to come.
And then wait in the Silence until the next one comes . . .
and then look over its shoulder.
Rinse and repeat.

Last night, I woke up a couple of times noticing thoughts about today, things that need to get done. I'm working on a couple of new projects, so there's a lot of thought activity. Instead of doing what I would've done years ago and becoming frustrated, I simply remembered to look through the thoughts, to look beyond them, to look over their shoulder. Actually, I heard that phrase for the first time, to look over a thought's shoulder back in 2013, reading a book by an author named Galen Sharp, *What Am I? A Study in Non-Volitional Living.*

Even if you're not having excessive, racing thoughts in this moment, this is an excellent Practice to engage in. Just as you wouldn't attempt to patch up a leaky roof in the midst of a rainstorm, trying to apply this practice during a mindstorm would be futile. Practice while the Sun/Son is shining in your heart and even when It appears to go behind the dark clouds, you'll still know It's (t)here. I see all of these practices as "break glass in case of emergencies" situation, but you have to be aware enough (you have to have practiced enough) to know the glass case and tool are available to you!

You're noticing many thoughts and inner turmoil that you label anxiety, upset, fear, or anger.

   Your inner dialogue could run something like this:

There are thoughts here.
Let me look past them.
Let me look over them.
Let me look through them.
The thoughts are coming,
but they're just another happening on the scene.
Just like the chair I'm sitting in,
Or this book I'm holding (or listening to),
or the phone in my hand,
thoughts are here but I don't have to pay attention to them.

That's the difference. That's what we're doing.

> "Be aware of the 'I' so intensely that no other thought can arise. If you are truly watchful, each thought will dissolve at the moment that it appears."
>
> **ANNAMALAI SWAMI**

You are not your thoughts. You are what is aware of them, which means you can let them be there while you place your attention elsewhere. You can rest in Presence, rest as Love while the thoughts come and go. When I am aware "my" thoughts are racing now, whether it's at night, or during the day, I pause and I find that place inside that is already quiet, untouched by thought activity, and then I rest there.

As you now know, (t)here's Love in that Silence. So it gives me a little bit of something to hang on to to or cling on to. So I pause, there's the Silence, and then in that Silence there is a Love and then I stay with the Love. And the more I stay with the Love, the more I remain as Love, the less loud the thoughts become, and the more pronounced and loud the Love is seen to be. The Love doesn't get louder or grow, but you just become more and more aware of it, and it truly drowns out and over-whelms everything. The great sages say that worldly appearances (including thoughts) become like the moon in daylight. Faint. Pale. Insig-nificant.

When you're aware of your Love, the world is seen to be unreal. And when you're aware of the world, you're unaware of Love. And so we're just shifting back and forth, back and forth all day. And eventually we start staying in and as this Love, and seeing Love everywhere we look.

Right now I'm looking at the ocean, but I feel Love. That's the differ-ence. It could be a person standing there and I'd be seeing a person and feeling Love. Knowing that the essence, the substance that makes that person, is that person, that is behind that person, that is more real than that person is Love. That's it. That's what's here. That's what you are. That's what I am. You're looking at God, but seeing these words.

You can make this into a formal practice and sit at some point today for just like five minutes. Set your phone timer and as thoughts come, every single thought, everyone that comes, look over its shoulder. Then there'll be a gap. There'll be a quiet. And then another thought will come and you'll look over its shoulder. And then there'll be a quiet, and you'll stay with the quiet, hang out in that space. And then another thought will come and you'll look over its shoulder. And you just do this. Do this for just five minutes today.

And then during the day too if you notice, if you're not too busy, you can practice looking over each thought's shoulders. Instead of just going with it and taking its hand and walking down the street and having a coffee together. Just let it go. Look over its shoulder, look past it. You can do this. You can try this. Establish a new relationship with thoughts. Until you know by feeling that they were never truly (t)here.

Silence is the Transcendent Moment, that Divine Instant, that Peaceful Stillness you notice when you drive under an overpass during a storm, or when your gas-saving engine shuts off at a stoplight, or when a too-loud TV or radio is shut off. The moment you notice the silence—that's Silence bowing to Silence, Love recognizing Love. I then love to continue recognizing the Silence as I drive back into the downpour, to continue feeling the Stillness us the engine rumbles back on, and to continue relishing the Love, the God that's still (t)here as the TV or radio or children or spouse do what they do. God is never disturbed I can't disturb Myself.

"Between two thoughts
there is an interval of no thought.
That interval is the Self, the Atman.
It is pure Awareness only."

———————

YOGA VASISTHA

Looking UP into Love (An Easy Way to Feel Love)

THE QUOTES

"We lost conscious unity with the Father and invented a new meaning for the word 'I.'

The word 'I' originally meant 'God.' The word 'I Am' really meant, 'God Is.' So when the word 'I' was spoken it was really 'I' uttering 'Itself.'"

———————

HERB FITCH

"I and the Father are one."
"All that Father has is mine."

———————

JESUS

THE PRACTICE

Close your eyes and place your hand over your heart.
While keeping your head level, look up behind your closed eyelids (as if at the ceiling).
Feel how the body feels . . . feel how the Soul feels, how God feels, in and AS the body.

Notice that when you look up behind closed eyes, you're looking up into Silence, into Infinity, into the Kingdom that you are misperceiving as darkness. Even if the mind had been noisy, in that moment, when you look up, you can hear the Love that the body is beginning to feel, again. Silence feels good.

BONUS PRACTICE

*Make a list of everything you think you need.
And then one by one, write, "I don't need _____, I only need the conscious awareness of the Love that 'I AM.'"*

*Once you have God,
you have everything you need.
Once you have the conscious awareness of Love,
you need nothing.
Feel the presence that you are, and know This to be the all.
When thoughts get loud, look up.
When anger comes to visit, look up.
When fear washes in, look up.
When you think you still have further to go to get HERE, look up.
Place your hand over your heart, close that body's eyes, and look up.*

Looking up interrupts the drama, the flow of thoughts, it interrupts "you," so you can hear the flow of Love. Its silence runs right next to the mind, right next to the world. To bring attention to this Divine Hearing, say inside, "Speak Father, your servant heareth" (1 Samuel 3 7-10), and listen, as if with bated breath. This is how you use that body like an antenna for Love, to hear into It, so that you may begin to vibrate like It, to again be an image of It.

> "When you feel a peaceful joy, that's when you are near truth."

ATTRIBUTED TO RUMI

There's something very powerful about this activity, using your eyes in this way, it slows the mind down. And when the mind has slowed down, it's very easy to become aware of your true Self, which is the same as my true Self, the Only Self, that only looks like you, and me, and them.

Whenever you notice a flurry of thoughts this week, close your eyes and look back up into Peace. Stay there awhile and bring It back down with you. You are Silent-Peace, not thoughts. When you think "I am 'me,'" you've gone just a little too far. The original declaration is simply, "I Am." You added your name, I added Nikki, we added our ages, our races, our politics, our religions and dogma. But there's just I Am with nothing following it. Nothing added. Just Love. You appear to be aware of it over there, and I appear to be aware of it over here, but it's self-aware, everywhere. It's been called the mind that was in Christ, Krishna consciousness, Buddha nature, but I call it Love.

> "One of God's Names is Love. He himself resides
> within all at every moment, everywhere."

ATTRIBUTED TO ANANDAMAYI MA

When you are aware of this Love, you are aware of having no needs. You are aware of being fulfilled, content, relaxed, softened, full, light. The shift from being unaware of Love to being Love-Conscious, simultaneously shifts you from the constant low-grade anxiety of "wanting," to "having." It's like you finally sit back in your seat and get comfortable. You relax your shoulders. You stop clenching your stomach, holding your breath. You're no longer waiting. You're being, you're Love.

I'm big on mantra and the repetition of prayer because of the way it puts my mind on one track. It makes it so that even when a million thoughts are present, there's one that's loudest. And I keep giving that my attention in the presence of all the others vying for attention, and eventually, there's only that one track and I can finally hear the Silence it's coming out of and going back into. I can finally feel that Silence, and I'm back to being Peaceful.

I've chanted Sanskrit mantras (like Hare Krishna, Hare Rama, and the Gayatri Mantra), and several short but powerful Bible verses, but there's one that kept me on track during my dark night of the soul in 2017: "I and the Father are one and all that the Father has is mine." Joel Goldsmith, the great teacher of the Infinite Way, introduced me to this gem. And whenever I'd find myself anxious or concerned, worried, or fearful, that verse would come up in me automatically, as if it was chanting me, praying me, keeping me going.

It was just announcing itself in me repeatedly throughout the day, especially in my most difficult moments. "I and the Father are one, and all that the Father has is mine. I and the Father are one." And I would sit with that in meditation quietly. "I and the Father are one. I is the Father. I is God." Which sounds like crazy English, right? Really bad English, but that's what that scripture is revealing. "I and the Father are one." That means that there's only one. So you don't even have to say I and the Father are one. There's just the Father. Appearing as you. Love appearing as you. That feeling of being "you" isn't "you"; It's Him. It always has been!

And because You are that Father appearing as you, you don't need anything. You have it all. The Kingdom is here. It is yours. "I and the Father are one. All that the Father has is mine."

Sit with that this week. Sit with and stay with the Love you find in the quick practice of looking up behind your closed eyelids and feeling down into the body, feeling down into that Love that initially announces itself as within you, but that quickly reveals that it is everywhere and that it is everything that appears to be.

And after you sit with that for a while, take out a sheet of paper and a pen. And write out the things that you think you need right now, the things that are missing from your life. I'll give you an example.

Let's say you need a new car. You need a new car because the one that you have is falling apart. So on that sheet of paper you'd write, "I don't need a new car. I need God-recognition." Or you can write, "I need the awareness of the I Am." You never need anything. You can say, "I don't need money. I need Love. I need to feel Love. I don't need a relationship, I need conscious recognition of the One, of the Father within, of the Christ Mind, of Buddha consciousness, of Krishna consciousness" (the Name doesn't matter, they are One, just as sol and zon are different ways to refer to the same sun). The name doesn't matter. You just need to experience It.

You have to experience the Love without names, without labels. And when you are living as That, That appears to take on the forms of what you need. It appears to become the miracles. It appears to be the healing that's necessary, not just for you and your family but for the world. Can't you see? All desires are limitations, but your present ones, which include simply having enough to care for your own family, to feed and clothe and heal your own family, are incredibly limiting. You're reading this book because you're here to clothe and feed the world. This Presence is big enough, powerful enough to encompass it all. You just have to realize it, and then you let it get to work without your consultation. You don't have to direct it. You don't have to tell it what to do. You don't have to pray to it with words. You don't have to direct it and send it at a particular person. You just have to be It, which means feel It without giving It any kind of concept. You become aware of this Love, and then you stay there and just marinate in and AS It.

You Love It,
you Love Love.
you just Love Love,
and then you watch what happens.
Because what happens is beautiful when you're here.
And you are here,
and you're living here now for a lot of the day,
and you're returning here to Love a lot of the day,
and the more you do,
the more of the day you're going to see unfold in miraculous ways.
Like I've mentioned before,
keep receipts.
Keep a note in your phone so that you always have something to go
back to when you're in a scary moment and you need faith.
And then you can make a note, "I don't need faith."
I need the presence of God,
the awareness that Love is (with) me. That whereon I stand is holy
ground.
That everywhere I am is church.
That everywhere I look, everywhere I see is Holy.
Everything is sacred.
You are Holy.
You are Divine.
Not the ego,
the I Am,
which is the same I Am that is here.
Not Nikki,
but the I Am before Nikki was,
the I am that'll be here after Nikki is gone.
We hold on to the awareness of This until we see that It's holding us,
and then we can drop the "us" and just stay with It.

Smiling into Love
(Instantly Shift into Love)

THE QUOTE

Go slowly, breathe, and smile.

———————

THICH NHAT HANH

THE PRACTICE

Half smile with parted lips,
exhale through that smile.
Practice holding a little half smile.
A Buddha smile.
A Mona Lisa smile.
Smile to stranger,
smile to nature,
smile to your smile,
smile to this Love.
Bow and smile to the presence of Peace within you.
When you notice the smile has faded,
return to the smile.
It will change everything.

Try This: *Smile into Love. Now allow your face to return to its normal resting position, but feel the smile that's still happening inside. Smile without smiling. This is your Eternal Smile. It's always "on" even when you forget to notice.*

I was at the airport recently waiting in line to speak with an attendant. As the line began to move, I reached for my bookbag at my feet and looked around at Love appearing as a busy gate. I immediately caught the eye of a woman beaming at me. I bowed gently and mouthed, "Hello," and she spoke back to me through her smile, loudly over the noise of the eager passengers, "You were smiling before you even turned around! It made me smile!"

Her smile further reinforced the one I wasn't even fully conscious of wearing in the moment! Smiling has become my new normal. I wore a frown through much of my teenage years, mostly as a defense mechanism to look unapproachable to keep my awkward self from having to communicate. Now I smile at everyone and no one. I'm smiling now. You should, too. Not a big, fake one, just allow all the corners of your mouth to turn up, slightly. Then notice how that turns up that GoOD feeling inside, subtly.

Try to hold this smile during the reading of this entire entry. And when you become aware that you've lost it, smile again. Anything that you're doing consciously like that becomes meditation, because it gives you something to come back to, to keep you here, to keep you rooted in the present moment. And so when you notice that you're no longer smiling, it's only because you were lost in thought again, but now you're lost in the smile. You're back.

I like to smile to Love, to smile to my inner being, to this Presence. Like the practice of Namaskar—folding my hands in front of me and bowing—you can bow to your inner Self, to that true Self, to the Love you feel and are. You could bow to a form of God out here. You can bow to a statue of Krishna, a murti of Krishna or Hanuman, an icon of Lord Jesus Christ and Mother Mary. You can bow to a person, to a teacher, to a Guru. But the true Guru, God, is this Love you're feeling within (there really is no within or without, or here or there, just Love). The Love that smile seems to stir.

This week, bow to That.
Honor That.
You can worship That.
That's true worship.
That's Darshan.

> "Worship nothing else other than the sense of presence, and when you are one with the sense of presence, then whatever is necessary by way of spiritual knowledge will sprout by itself."
>
> ———————
>
> **ATTRIBUTED TO NISARGADATTA MAHARAJ**

In Hinduism, they talk about being in the presence of a great saint or teacher and having them lay eyes on you, to witness you, to be aware of you. But for me, as soon as I feel this Presence, I know that it is God. I know I am seen, that I'm receiving and giving Darshan. I see myself as God sees me. Not as Nikki, but as Her, as the I Am. Not, I am God, but a felt-knowing that "I Am" IS God. This Presence is God.

> "Come what may today I am going to smile. Everything is going to vanish and disappear, so what'? Let me be at least happy. Smile this very moment and enjoy my very breath if not nothing else."
>
> ———————
>
> **SRI SRI RAVI SHANKAR**

This presence that you feel where you are, that you know as "I Am _____ (your name)," That's God. Just drop your name, drop all the demographics, and stay with the I . . . Am . . . remain as the silence that follows "am." That's You.

And it's your mother, father, grandma, children, dog, or even that squirrel outside, and anyone you can think of, living or passed on, that Presence looks like them for a while, and then it looks like something else. Right now, it's looking like these words, those hands, it's sounding like that breath, this Silence, this Love.

Being aware of (and as) this Love is your purpose, and smiling is a very effective permission slip to sliding into the awareness of It. When you smile at a stranger, you activate that in them. You see them smile back. And even those that do not, it's not a smile wasted. It's a seed planted. I smile at every individual, every being because I feel myself there. I know that this Love is there, too. I feel Love where I see them. The same Love that's here, I know it's there, and so I can't help but smile, a knowing, loving smile.

Don't hurry today. Don't rush this week. Every time you notice that frantic energy—when your shoulders are up and your stomach is tight, and your breath is fast or you're holding it (like we often do when we're stressed—the next time you're lost in thought, notice that you were also holding your breath!). Become aware enough to notice and to stop that cycle and to interrupt it with a smile, to interrupt your ego with God over and over again as often as you can remember. Smile, and exhale through it. See through the seeming challenge. Move through the seeming challenge to the Love that's here and awaits.

In This Moment, Be Love

Be still (in Silence, in felt-Love, in My Name), and know that I Am (is) God.
Wake up as that Stillness, the Silence, the Love, the Name that is always,
already there, and know It to be your Self.
The Infinite appearing as the finite, but still Infinite.
God looking like a person, but still God.
Love

THE QUOTE

"I will go before you and make the crooked places straight."

———————

ISAIAH 45:2-3, NKJV

"Be silent. Be still . . . Let your God—Love you.

———————

EDWINA GATELEY, "LET YOUR GOD LOVE YOU"

THE PRACTICE

Stand up into Love,
and gently lift your head, your chin, your face as if you're warming
yourself in the sun that's been covered for far too long.
Smile.

Breathe deep.

Warm yourself in this Love.

Know this Love as the "I"—the One that goes before you to smooth your path.

*Know that "I" goes before you to make the crooked places straight. Feel the **Love** that goes before you to smooth the path.*

Today, you're going to stay aware of the Stillness that was Here before "you" could get still. Before you could sit still. Before you could practice being still. You're going to stay aware of this Original Stillness, even as that body is active. Even while that mind is running, this Silence is running. And because you're aware of It, It's going to appear to take you far—right into those experiences you've been wanting, into this elevated way of living. But in order to keep going, to keep rising, you have to stay Here, too. You can't leave Here. You have to be Here, Now, to get "there," that's the paradox. Being this Stillness while in motion. Being this Love, even while fearful. Being Surrender even when "you" can't.

What is the "I" that goes before you to smooth out the way to prevent the problem so that there isn't even an issue when you arrive?

So that there is no problem?

What is the "I" that does this?

Ask yourself this question. And feel the answer, that Silence that seems to start in your right ear.

In a moment, close your eyes and relax your body. Come into the moment fully, recognizing that it's not even a moment, it's just Presence appearing as a moment, just Love.

And then feel Love for the breathing that's happening.
Feel Love for any ambient sounds, whatever you hear where you
appear to be, Love that.
It's not disturbing you.
It is what it is,
it's happening and it could not be any other way.
Your thoughts are happening and they could not be any other way.
You don't stop them,
you don't try to stop them,
you can't stop them,
but you can Love them.
Love your thoughts as they come and go.
If there's any pain in that body, Love that.
Any tension or tightness, feel Love for that tension.
It's really just Love appearing as tension, know this and feel this.
We Love every sensation,
every object,
every thought.
And then we realize there's only Love,
there's just Love and you are that Love.
Only Love is left, only You are here;
everything is dissolved in this Love, which is formless and
invisible.
Inevitable.
You can't see it, although it takes on many forms,
you can't touch it,
It can never be hurt.
It doesn't have an age or a weight or a name; you can't describe It.
But you know you can be still and know This,
because you are This.
And This that you're aware AS right now,
is the "I" that goes before that body that you think you are to make

the crooked places straight.
This Love is that "I" that I am.
It's the "I" that you are truly.
And when you're in flow with It,
in flow as It,
that body is carried to where it can be of service, powerful service.
It's carried to where it can be Loved.
It's carried to where it can prosper, blossom, fruit.

But because of the conscious awareness of this Love, that body knows that the fruit isn't the point, that the comforts of this life, they're not the point. **That this Love is the point,** this Love is all that's ever needed. And as long as this Love is remembered, everything is here. It comes into your experience exactly when it is needed and not a moment before. Your ego might think something was needed yesterday for its security, its safety, and its comfort, but It can't show up until the moment it's needed.

Think about the last time you felt you were in too deep. The last time you couldn't see a way out, and so you began painting your own doors, frustrated when they wouldn't open. Your doors are here. And they're already open. You've always been taken care of, you know that. And whatever you're going through now, it's no different. The solutions will come, the opportunities will be seen, the right person will reach out. But when they do, you'll recognize them or it for what it is, Love.

Love appearing as a solution,
Love appearing as a person,
Love appearing as a new income stream.
But there's just Love, just this Love and it's all you have to practice.
Be with It, commune with It, abide in It, let It abide in you,
let It go before you to smooth the road, to make the crooked places
straight.

How comforting is that?
To know that this felt-Love you are sitting in and AS right now is
already at your office?
Already at that meeting, appearing as that meeting you're
dreading?
It's already on the next day of the week?

It's already next year? It's already five years, ten years from now? All you have to do is, in this moment, be Love. And in this moment, be Love. And in this moment, be Love. In every moment you're choosing, you have a choice: you can either be the person you think you are or you can be Love. And I can assure you that if you make that decision to be Love over and over until you recognize that you never had any choice (this is what you are, you just had a mistaken belief that you are this person only), you'll know beyond a shadow of a doubt that It's been carrying you, that It's been providing for you because It is You.

How would It not care for itself or provide for Itself? That makes no sense, right? You don't have to ask your Self for anything, but you have to be That to receive.

> "You don't have to ask the sun for warmth, or for a tan, or for light, you just go and stand in it. Go stand in the sun, you'll get your warmth, you'll get the tan, you'll have all the light that you need, but you can't be asking for all that and begging for all that inside with your curtains drawn and the lights out sitting in the corner."
>
> **JOEL GOLDSMITH**

You have to stand as That.
Right now,
stand up,
lift your head just a little bit as if you are facing the sun/Son and
receiving the warmth from It.
Feel Love on your face and throughout that body as you would if
you were standing in the sun,
feeling its rays on your face and on your body: feel Love, knowing
that this Love that you can
feel right now is the I that goes before you to make the crooked
places straight.
It's already solved the problems,
the problems you don't even know existed or could have existed.
They're finished,
they're done.
Solutions that you feel you're needing right now,
they're already there.
When you get there, they'll be there waiting for you.
Whether it's a house you need or money you need, an opportunity
or a contract you need, it's already there.
You get there by being Love,
knowing this Love,
and when you know this Love,
you relax.
You get there with this warm, gentle, loving relaxation,
not with stress, intention, worry, and wheel spinning.
We get there with Love, relaxed-Love.
Love is the bridge.
Love is our car.

Meditation, which is conscious contact with Love, solves all
problems.

Open Your Eyes as Love

THE QUOTES

"Close your eyes, fall into the Presence of Love, stay (t)here."

_____

RUMI

"Real vision is eyeless."

_____

ANANDAMAYI MA, *MATRI VANI (WORDS OF THE MOTHER)*

"The experience of Self is only love, which is seeing only love, hearing only love, feeling only love, tasting only love, and smelling only love, which is bliss."

_____

SRI RAMANA MAHARSHI

"Remember: if you want to make progress on the path and descend to places you have longed for, the important thing is not to think much, but to Love much, and so to do whatever best awakens you to Love."

_____

ST. TERESA OF AVILA, *THE INTERIOR CASTLE*

THE PRACTICE

Once an hour or as often as you can remember,
close your eyes as the person you take yourself to be,
and open them AS Love.
Bring the Loving Silence you find inside,
out into the world.
Feel Love where you see people.
Let the Love replace the scene.

Six. Sometimes seven. That's how many books were open on my bed or strewn across my desk, being skimmed, highlighted, and re-read at any given time in my journey to realizing and appreciating where I had actually never left. This Love I had always been.

This week I'm calling you to put the books down. Even this one. Get the goods and then get on with feeling God. You are the book, you are the Truth, and unless you read, feel, and know your Self, you'll keep pretending to be something you're not. When I felt the call to put the books down, that's when the biggest leaps were made. It's like I couldn't bear to read another word (you know the feeling). I'd close the book and vow to simply practice what I knew to be true for the next week or two, and what was once only something read in a book (and sounded true), became a moment-to-moment experience. What was once second nature became first. Seeds would sprout and the lesson would become an encounter, something alive, something that could now actually be shared with the rest of my Self (the seeming "others"). It doesn't matter the book or the religion or the teacher, they're all pointing to This. You can either practice This now, or practice It thirty years from now, but you will have to practice It until you're being It effortlessly, gracefully.

> "Talk little. Reading and talking create interference in the mind. Too much discussion is not the way."
>
> ———————
>
> ATTRIBUTED TO NEEM KAROLI BABA

So let's be It now.
In a moment you'll close that body's eyes,
And feel Love wrap its arms around that body,
gently swaying it side to side.
Right to left, left to right.
Allow that face to smile.
Allow Love to announce Itself more and more within that body's
heart,
within that body's being.
Allow Love, the feeling of Love,
to replace that body entirely.
Your true body is Love.
It's your indestructible,
unborn,
never-dying,
invisible light body,
and that same Love,
that is where you are,
is here, where I am,
and everywhere in between.
It's everywhere, always,
in every moment,
even the ugly ones,
even the dark ones.
And now you've been awakened,

you've been alerted to your purpose.

Being This, consciously, is your purpose.

You can take a moment to remember who you are,

what you are,

no matter where you are,

just by doing a simple reset, closing your eyes for a moment, and

feeling God where you are, where that body appears to be, where

the world appears to be, feeling Love and knowing Love, where

your coworker appears to be, where your spouse appears to be.

The eyes report people,

but you feel their truth,

their Essence.

You feel Love where they are seen.

And so you go about your day today and every day,

and you get lost in the world as usual,

but at least once an hour,

set an alarm on your phone.

And when it goes off, if you have the ability, if you're in an

environment where it's safe to do so,

just close your eyes for a moment,

just a few seconds,

and listen for Silence.

Listen for Love just beyond the sound of the chime

Allowing the chiming or ringing to carry you into the Silence.

And as you open your eyes,

You bring that Love out into the world,

and you feel It where you see the world,

and then you get lost in the world,

and you do the things,

and then the chime goes off again,

and you close your eyes just for a moment,

and you feel your truth,

and then you open your eyes,
and you bring that Truth back out.
And you do this over and over and over.
You do this until you don't have to close your eyes anymore,
or set the alarm anymore, only Love is here, always,
and you know It as your Self.

> "The eyes can be closed or open as one finds convenient. It is not the eyes that see. There is one who sees through the eyes."
>
> ———
>
> **SRI RAMANA MAHARSHI**

Shut those eyes like a reset. Open them, and be who you are.
Let Love open those eyes. You close your eyes as that human.
Like right now, I'm closing my eyes as Nikki, but opening
them as Love. Close your eyes now as that human and open
them as Love.

Hold Love's Hand

THE QUOTE

"If you knew who walked beside you at all times, on the path that you have chosen, you could never experience fear or doubt again."

_____

WAYNE DYER, ADAPTED FROM *A COURSE IN MIRACLES*

THE PRACTICE

Personalize that boundless, formless Love as the presence of your transitioned Loved one. For me, It's my Grandma Maxine. I take her hand in the morning, and I don't let It go. I don't let Love go. I practice holding Love's hand and letting It guide me through my challenges, ups and downs, during the day, until I recognize that even when I seem to let go of Its hand, or forget, It's still holding mine. Love is still holding me.

Try this every morning and evening this week, and watch how easier it is to stay aware of Love!

"You still don't know who walks behind you."

_____

NEEM KAROLI BABA (HEARD FROM WITHIN MY BEING)

This powerful practice knocks the legs out from under any worry, concern, or fear you may have. It will keep you remembering that you're on the path, and that you're safe, and that this Presence is God, It's consciousness, It's Awareness, It's Love, It's everything, including You, when you know who you are. And if that's the case, then there's nothing or no one to be afraid of, there's nothing to worry about, nothing to think about. You can rest. Abide. Dissolve. Even if just for this timeless moment.

In the beginning, when I first started practicing the presence of God or practicing the presence of Love, it was easier and quite a bit more powerful and more palpable to be able to personalize the Love. Even though it's never been localized or personal, that's how we experience It and so It's easiest to conceptualize this practice that way. Practicing this formless, boundless, infinite Love. Invisible Love is great, but It's slippery, right? Elusive. So in the beginning I gave It the form of my Grandma Maxine. She passed away in Dec 2015, and I remember sitting in meditation one day and feeling that Love bubble up, which did not happen as often then as It does now. It's never not here, now, and although It was never not there back then, I didn't turn to It often. But whenever I did, It was amazing. And it felt like something that I was doing, something that I was efforting and holding and remembering. And then life would rush back in and I'd be like, "Where has this Love gone?" And so it was challenging, but when I made that invisible, formless Love, the presence, the Spirit of my Grandma Maxine, and taking it a step further, her holding my hand, that's when it became a little easier to practice.

Because if my grandma were here in this room with me, I would hold her hand and I would never let it go. I would keep holding her hand. I would never forget because I'd be so happy to see her and to know that she was here again. You see that?

So first, I feel Love.

And for me, I would say, "Grandma's holding my hand. She's walking with me. She's with me. She's guiding me through these scary scenes in this Nikki movie, she's reminding me with her presence, with the felt

Love, that everything is okay. That everything is as it should be, even though it doesn't appear to be, even though it does not look like it. She's with me and she's guiding me."

And so this week's practice is for you to take the hand of your Loved one, someone who is dear to you who has transitioned, and make this Loving Presence them, and hold their hand all day. Don't let their hand go. If it helps, envision, imagine, visualize that person, your person, and feel the Love that you have for them. Let that Love rush up and announce itself where you are. Feel the Love you have for them purely.

And now drop the image of them. You don't need the image anymore. Just stay with the Love. Feel that Love, and know that that's your Loved one with you today and this week energetically holding your hand. It's not a belief. This is felt-Faith. You feel the Presence, and because you feel the Presence you know are safe.

Turn to that Love and say "thank you."

Turn to It and say "I Love you."

> "They say that I am dying but I am not going away.
> Where could I go? I am here."
>
> ——————
>
> **SRI RAMANA MAHARSHI**

"Safe" isn't even the word because that would imply that you need to be protected from something, from some other power. Only Love is here, and you are Love.

Where Is Love Now?

THE QUOTES

"Only for to-day need you try to keep close our contact. Only for the present moment are you held responsible. To-morrow, yea, even the next hour is yet unborn. So you see, after all the task is not such a hard one. Hold fast to My hand now, this very moment feel its tender touch and verily you shall not be left alone in the next hour, day or month."

———————

EVA BELL WERBER, *IN HIS PRESENCE*

"Why should you worry about the future? You don't even know the present properly. Take care of the present and the future will take care of itself."

———————

SRI RAMANA MAHARSHI

THE PRACTICE

As often as you can remember this week, ask, "Where is Love now? And then feel It right where you are, and know that this is all you have to do. You don't have to feel It in the future. You can only ever feel It now, and know that because you feel It now, the future is taken care of.

> "Buddha never says, 'Stop thinking.' He says, 'Breathe consciously.' Automatically, thinking will stop; you cannot both think and breathe consciously. When a thought comes into your mind, your attention is withdrawn from the breathing. A single thought and you have become unconscious of the breathing process."

> OSHO

In this moment,
now, as I'm bringing your attention to it,
you are aware of your breath,
you are fully here.
And the opportunity is that in this next seeming moment,
here you are.
And so it's always only ever one conscious breath.
That's all you can take.
Future ones are imagination.
Right now, where is that?
How can you be conscious in the future?
How can be conscious in the past?
You can only be conscious of this breath,
and of this one,

and of this one. If you're thinking about how difficult it's going to be for you to be conscious of your breath when you get to the office, or how you can be conscious of your breath tomorrow when you have to go on a lunch date with somebody from work, or when you have to have that difficult but necessary conversation, you're already not conscious of the breath now in this moment because you're thinking about a future moment that has not arrived yet or may never arrive. It's impossible to be conscious of that breath in the future.

And when you're thinking about it, you're not conscious of the only one you can be aware of now and now.

And so it's not hard. It's not difficult.

You don't have to be aware of Love forever.

That's a heavier lift than being aware of Love now.

Can you see the difference there?

And I know you've done it. I've done it. I did it for years. Setting that goal, "I'm going to be aware of Love all day." I still do that because it's fun, but it's impossible (because the one trying to stay aware of Love isn't actually here . . . it's a thought, too!).

But if you can remember, "I just have to be aware of Love now," and then feel It. You can even say, "Where is Love now?" Especially when it feels like you can't be aware of it or you've lost it. Where is Love now? And listen for It. Look for It. Behind closed eyes, or eyes wide open, not blinking, staring through whatever appears to be in front of that body.

And there it is.

And even if you can't feel It yet, don't be frustrated.

For now, trust me that It is there.

Maybe all you can be aware of is the Silence or Quiet that follows that question when you say, "Where is Love now?" Just that Silence that follows the question is GoOD enough. Soon, with Grace, you'll be aware of the Love in that Silence, you'll be aware of Love as that Silence, Silence as the Love. But in the meantime, just keep bringing the question back and listening to the Silence that follows the question. As if that Silence is holding a secret you desperately need to hear. Attentive listening.

Where is Love right now?

Where is Love now?

*When I ask that question, my eyes cut to the right, like I'm
listening for the answer with my right ear. But I'm not listening
for words, I'm listening for a feeling. And then The Feeling
comes, but it's not a feeling that's actually coming because it
never leaves. My attention seems to come and my attention
seems to leave it, but this Love is steady, It's constant. It is us.
It's the awareness of every single seeming moment you've had.
The attention flickers but the Love stands.*

*Just keep returning to that question,
And feeling the Silence that follows and just staying there as long
as you can.
Do this at least once an hour,
But if you have time to dedicate to this,
for five to ten minutes of just sitting with that question and every
time thoughts come to try to drive you away,
bring the question back up and sit in the Silence that follows and
repeat the question as needed.
Not like a mantra.
Just use it as a guide back to where your feet are.
Back to Now.
Back at One.*

*Even though there's no "you" to sustain this Love that's always
already "on," you still think you're a "you" who hasn't gotten "It"
yet, a "you" who's "almost there" . . . and so because of that, join
me for part 2—Sustaining Love, or feeling It constantly (even
though all you ever have to do is feel It Now, and now and now
and now).*

PART TWO

Sustaining Love

Spend your whole day in Love.
The same way you feel when you're in human love,
but all of that directed at God.
There's no ghosting here,
no flexing here,
no hurt feelings here,
not even conversation, here—
like when you're with someone real special,
and you can just sit with them in the silence,
and it doesn't feel awkward,
there's no struggle to think of something to say to fill the space,
'cause the space is so full,
Love is so full.
This is how you sit with God,
AS God.
Hey, God.

"It is by God's Grace that you think of God."

_____

"It is easy to bear the heat of fire and likewise
it is possible to tread the edge of the sword.
But to sustain an unchanging love is a most difficult business."

_____

KABIR

Week 16

Dissolving Bad Moods in Love

THE QUOTE AND THE PRACTICE

Just as the boundless and expanded everywhere "I" of you and God are one, this week, the quote and practice are one:

"This moment couldn't be any other way," or
"This mood, how I feel right now, couldn't be any other way."
"Notice your negative or heavy mood but don't try to change it.
Think of it like weather.
You can't change it.
You wouldn't even try to change it.
You just shelter in place.
This mood is inner weather.
Let it blow through.
You just feel and be Love while the inner storm is raging.
See through the storm to the Love that's actually there."

––––––––––

MEDITATION INSPIRED BY *A COURSE IN MIRACLES*

I woke up yesterday on the wrong side of the bed and that looks different than it used to look. I'm very sensitive, more aware of the moving energy we call emotion, so there was the awareness of a feeling of "offness," "agitation," "irritability," "fatigue." There was a desire to remain in bed. Nothing in particular was going on. No new responsibilities, no new problems, just "inner weather."

It was also a rainy day yesterday, and that's what's inspiring me to share. When I interviewed Tracee Ellis Ross and Rhonda Ross for my podcast for the Ram Dass network, New Growth, we talked about these moods that come seemingly uncaused, with Tracee referring to them as inner weather. Sometimes, you can point to a cause, but either way, it's weather inside, just like weather happens outside. Some days it's sunny and clear, and other days it's gray and cloudy. Some days you wake up sunny and clear, and other days you might wake up sleepy, groggy, overwhelmed, anxious, fearful, but you can't do anything about that.

Note: It's not even your fear! It's not your anxiety. You've tuned into human fear, picking up ancient thoughts and feelings of survival, and have claimed them as your own. You can just as easily tune into Divine Love. You can just as easily tune into Silence, or Stillness, or even the Sound of God's Name (see Week 20).

And the danger, what we run into, especially in this seeming "self-help" arena, is trying to make that body-mind feel better, to make your character feel better. "I have to get out of this mood, out of this funk," and that ultimately creates more tension. Our work is seeing through the storm, knowing that the storm couldn't be any other way. There's so much power in that. When I woke up yesterday, still, for a few seconds, the thought came, "Ugh, I don't want to feel like this. I know this and I don't want to feel this way."

But I intentionally got up, did my spiritual practice, even though I wasn't feeling blissful about it. And I carried out my responsibilities. I recorded for Love appearing as the world, as you, and I wrote in my journal, and I went to work—writing and Zoom calls all day. At about, I'd say, five or six o'clock, that energy was still there. It was definitely not a sunny day; I was very aware that it was not a sunny day, but there was the constant recognition that the storm inside couldn't be any other way. And that I, as Awareness, as Consciousness, as Love, had to continue to be consciously That while Nikki was showing up stormy, while Nikki was experiencing a rainy day. Rainy day and Nikki may have been appearing, the clouds were there—but Love was still (t)here, shining.

> "When things in you move, you don't have to move with them."
>
> ADYASHANTI

I was feeling/being Love while the storm was blowing through Nikki—not trying to shift Nikki out of feeling sad or low or tired, just recognizing the Love that's (t)here, also. Seeing through the storm, seeing through the clouds to the Love. That's it; that's all I did. And by eight o'clock that night, I had received some of the best news of the whole month. And I don't think it's a coincidence, nothing is. I stayed with the practice. I stuck with it. And that's major because if you came up in the early Law of Attraction teachings like I did, you'd think that feeling bad means you're attracting bad. If you're feeling negative, expect negativity. Inner storms bring about outer storms. While this line of thought isn't destructive (thought has no power) in the way you may have been taught, it can be distracting. **"Bad" moods come and go. "Good" moods come and go. But what sees them coming and going?** What is aware of the changes in the weather, in the pressure, in the sunshine or seeming lack thereof (Spoiler: even when it appears to be night, the sun is still shining, even when it's cloudy, the sun is still here.) YOU. The way your body feels, the moods that come and go, have no effect on what you are or on what you'll appear to manifest in a future-now.

You being present in each moment,
even during the moments of upset,
being present as Love,
Love manifests itself.
The Love seems to become more Love,
It looks and feels like more Love, more health, more life, more
abundance, more to smile about.
Just cling to Love.
Hold, stay, sit at the feet of Love,
hold Love's hand,
and Namaskar your way to Love.
All the practices, do whatever it takes to stay as Love,
even when that body is upset.
And you'll see all is well, all is always very well.
It's all God, it's all good.

So the practice this week is to see any mood, even if it's a minor little annoyance, as inner weather. You'll see it come, you'll see it go. And while it is present, it could not be any other way. And your only job in that moment is not to make the person that you think you are feel better, you just feel for Love, too. You could even ask, "'Is Love here, too'? The storm is here, the pain, upset, or worry is here, but can I feel Love, too?" Feel Love while the storm is happening. That's it.

   If a thought about the past comes, remember, "that couldn't have happened any other way." If a thought about something you said comes or wish you would've said but didn't: "That couldn't have happened any other way. What was said was exactly the only thing that could've been said in that moment."

Remember these words, remember what I'm saying. And next time you feel upset, which will happen today—we all do, every single day, up and down—remember that this moment couldn't be any other way. The storm is here. I don't have to do anything about that, but I have to be awake enough to be who I really am while the storm is happening.

I was on a flight recently and the announcement for the initial descent had just been made. I'm usually an aisle girl, but I was seated by the window, looking out over a thick layer of clouds beneath the plane. We were flying into NYC and I was trying to peer through the clouds to see exactly over what part of the city we were, hoping to recognize some of the buildings, waiting to see the ground. But there were so many clouds. I was super attentive, just waiting, watching, blinking only when necessary, almost holding my breath, waiting to be able to peek through the clouds to see what was (t)here. This made me smile because I recognized that my spiritual practice is just like this—seeing through my inner clouds, waiting to become aware of the Ground, the Love that I truly Am. So I was peering through the clouds that were obstructing the city, the skyline, and then finally there was the opening, and I could see—we were coming in over the Statue of Liberty. And I said and felt, "Ahhhhh, freedom. Freedom."

Another airport example: I was about to miss an international flight back home, and I stopped, closed my eyes for a second, and just saw through that frustration and anxiety until I could feel the Love that I am, again. And of course, I got on a flight and got to where I was going without missing a beat. You just stop in whatever moment you're in that's stressful. And for me, it's like a listening. I'm listening for the feeling of Love in the chaos, in the stress. And there It is.

Or sometimes it's like I can feel, in the pit in my stomach, that feeling you get when you're on a roller coaster; that's the same kind of feeling I have when I'm anxious. And I can become aware of that like a ball of energy, while feeling into the space that's next to it. Comfort is right next to the discomfort. Bliss is right here next to, and even pervading, the pain. Look again. Feel again. "Is Love here, too?" In the Silence, you feel the "Yes." You'll feel the discomfort in your chest or stomach, and then you'll become aware of and AS the space that's surrounding that seeming energy. You'll find that space is free and open and airy and Love. It's full of Love. The Love isn't being seemingly drowned out by the density of that other energy. The density of that other energy is happening in and as Love, too, but it's harder to know that and see that. So you just feel into the space right next to it, and there's the Love. And then that density dissolves. It turns back into Love. This works for physical pain, too. You feel the pain, and then feel for what's right next to it. It couldn't be any other way.

You couldn't be anywhere else.

But I still thank you for being here.

I love you!

> "This place where you are right now
> God circled on a map for you
> He has bowed there, knowing you were coming."
>
> ———
>
> HAFIZ

Know that where you are right now is where you are meant to be. You couldn't be anywhere else doing anything else. Your purpose is to wake up to Love in the midst of whatever your present life circumstances are. No matter how challenging they are, because as Dr. Bruce Davis says, "Love found in the midst of great difficulty, is Love found forever." And I'm living proof!

You are built for this. God chose you. Step into It. Know this, feel this, smile, and be Love.

Stepping Into Love
(Love Steps)

This practice will help you abide in Love as you cross the bridge from your old life into the new one, the real one. New life, same Love. The Rebirth into and as Spirit.

THE QUOTE

"Be fully aware of your own being and you will be in Bliss consciously. Because you take your mind off yourself and make it dwell on what you are not, you lose your sense of well-being."

_____

NISARGADATTA MAHARAJ

THE PRACTICE

Listen to an uplifting song, challenge yourself to feel Love until the song ends. Loop the Love, forever.

> "If a man had no more to do with God than to be thankful, that would suffice"
>
> ──────────
>
> **MEISTER ECKHART**

Select a song from the following list (or a song choice of your own without words, that is uplifting), and find a room where you can be alone.

1. Press play (headphones are preferable).

2. Stand in the middle of the room, fold your hands in front of you (Namaskar), bow ever so slightly, and close your eyes (if you can safely—ensure you have enough room). Using that body as an antenna for the Divine, you will automatically become aware of Love. It's a humbling posture. (See part 1, practice 1.)

3. Take slow, little steps while repeating "thank you" inwardly, feelingly, opening your eyes on occasion to check where you are in the room, so that you don't bump into anything. (I take baby steps in little circles, very slowly.)

4. Practice Love during the entire song, feeling GoOD in every step. Try to stay aware of Love for the WHOLE song. And when thoughts come, let them go and return to the "Thank you" mantra, the beautiful music, and the Love. Repeat the song at least once, if you have time!

IMPORTANT: Let each step be taken in the feeling, the energy or vibration, of Love. Do as Thich Nhat Hanh says and KISS THE FLOOR with each and every step. You'll know you're doing it right if you are smiling! Let the music point you back to your inner smile, to the Love inside, to the Love that you are. Imagine that each step is one taken across the bridge from your old life to your new one. New life, same Love.

My favorite is first, but I Love them all.

Any beautiful song, without words preferably, will work!

"I Giorni" (Live) by Ludovico Einaudi

"River Flows in You" by Yiruma

"Pacheelbel Meets U2" by Jon Schmidt

"With or Without You" (Live) by The Piano Guys

"A Thousand Years" by The Piano Guys

"On the Way to the BeLoved" by Karuna

*Because you take your mind off Love, and focus it on the body,
mind, and all of its projected problems, you lose your sense of
contentment*
The remedy?
Stay aware of the I Am,
stay aware of Love,
and you'll be happy twenty-four/seven.
You must keep your attention on Spirit, on God, on Me,
*To experience the happiness that transcends what you think of
as happiness.*
This is the "happy" that's "happy" for no reason.

It's not tied to anything material—to anything that can rush, die, or abandon.

But when you abandon yourself to It, you'll find It to be the bridge to a life that better reflects what you've found inside, what you've felt yourself to be.

As soon as you finish reading these instructions, find a place where you can close the door and walk around and not be bothered—in order to not feel self-conscious doing this. You're going to play the song of your choice in headphones, or out loud if you can. And while it's playing, you're going to repeat the mantra"Thank you." Simply say, "Thank you, thank you, thank you," out loud, softly, humbly, full of loving gratitude. Or you can think it internally, loud, excitedly, as if you just got something that you've been wanting for ten years. I like to do the internal excited voice, the excited "thank-yous" inside. Even more powerfully, you can practice Namaskar while you're doing this. You can bow gently and close your eyes (opening them only to make sure you aren't walking toward a piece of furniture).

> **"The best things in life are unseen; that's why we close our eyes when we kiss, cry, and dream."**
>
> ———————
>
> **OFTEN ATTRIBUTED TO HELEN KELLER**

This practice uses music, the body's posture, and the little steps to hold you in Love. One song lasts around 3–5 minutes, so I recommend you repeat it at least twice. These Love steps (or happy feet!) are more powerful than you think. I'm seated right now, but I'm moving the way I move when I walk, even though I'm typing. Swaying gently, feeling Love in the sway.

And if you're consciously feeling Love for ten minutes, even for just five minutes, you're changing your life. You're changing your lived experience. I did this for a few months, every single day, fifteen minutes a day. And now I live where I live with the people who I live with, surrounded by Love. It changed very quickly, very powerfully, very predictably, scientifically. And I do feel that this practice was one of the main bridges that got me here. So give it a try. Do it right now before you launch into the rest of your day. If you can't walk in little circles or around a room while listening, at least sit and listen. Use the music, let it guide you into Love and do your thank-yous inside. Say "Thank you" to the Love, Namaskar to the feeling of Love, Namaskar to this God within you that you are aware of. Thank God that you are aware of God within you as yourself. Say thank you to that knowledge. Say thank you to the beautiful music.

Say thank you for having a moment to be able to practice this. That itself is a luxury. This is the first sign of abundance.

And thoughts will come. Thoughts to pull you out of this practice— thinking about what you need to do later, what you should be doing at that moment instead of walking around in circles with your eyes closed, say- ing, "Thank you," along with a piece of classical music. It will feel like you're not being productive. Your mind will throw up lots of things to scare you, to make you anxious. Let those thoughts go and return to your thank yous. Return to the sound of the music. Return to the sound of the inner thank- you. You can even begin to say thank you out loud (if you weren't) if your mind is very noisy, to bring you back to the practice. And then as your mind quiets back down, you can return to your inner thank-yous. And the inner thank-you is powerful because if you're shouting it like I'm suggest- ing, that smile, that inner Love becomes so present that you become that.

And when you are fully aware of that, the thoughts just dissolve. The thoughts are not there. And even when they do come, you're not at- tracted to them because the Love is so attractive. You don't care about the thoughts so you stay in the Love effortlessly. And then when the thought comes that does pull you out, you just go back to saying it out loud if you need to, "Thank you, thank you," until it gets quiet. Go back to your inner thank-yous excitedly, until that Love is palpable and you stay in Love. And when you're in Love truly, there are no thoughts, just Love appearing as thoughts.

There's only Love here. God's song.

Notice that one of the first places you can become aware of this subtle vibration emanating is in your feet. It's why people rush to touch the feet of Saints and elders in India. Simply become aware of and keep returning your attention to Love where your feet appear to be.

The Practice That Changed My Life (The Most Powerful Mantra)

"God is constantly chanting a mantra to call you. Can you hear it? Listen constantly. Repeat it with Him with Love, constantly.

'And as I come to you, Holy Father, protect them by your Name, that which you gave Me, so that they may be one, just like Us.'"

JESUS (JOHN 16:11), VICTOR N. ALEXANDER, *ARAMAIC SCRIPTURE*

THE QUOTES

"If you do Japa mantra, you'll always be benefited. You will never lose anything."

ATTRIBUTED TO ANANDAMAYI MA

"Those who sing the praise of Him are no longer ordinary men trapped in the world."

UNKNOWN

"That student unto whom the Lord becomes merciful chants the Lord's name and wins the game of life."

GURU RAM DAS JI

"Knowingly or unknowingly, consciously or unconsciously, in whatever state of mind a man utters God's 'name,' he acquires the merit of such utterance."

SRI RAMAKRISHNA

"By repeating the name of Ram [God], everything is brought to completion."

NEEM KAROLI BABA

"All names given to God have the same power. You can reach your destination by taking any name you like. The more intense your sadhana, the quicker you reach Him. Take it lightly and you take more time."

ANANDAMAYI MA

THE PRACTICE

Pick a mantra and ride it Home.

Or better stated—

Let a mantra chant you into the recognition that you have always been Home (dreaming you were elsewhere), that you've always been Me.

The repetition of a Name of God, or Japa, was my main practice for years. I attribute a lot of the rapid deepening and rising to that. I attribute my ability to share with you here and every morning on the podcast to that. The idea to share this Love in the form of a podcast every morning came from this practice (in addition to deciding to wake up early enough to be able to execute it, to commit to it, to commit to sitting in the presence of Love every day). The serendipitous events that led up to the sharing of this book came from this practice. I've often said that chanting is like the FastPass at Disney—when you're not doing this practice, you're still in line, you're still moving forward, just slower, but when you're waking up before the sun every morning, chanting God's Name, the line moves swiftly, because you're the only one in line. Lessons that would've taken you years to learn, you learn in months, in weeks—you burn up karma fast. In Love, there are no thoughts, there is no old or new karma, and Success in this life is inevitable and comes quickly.

The most powerful mantra is the one you keep coming back to. The one that helps you keep recognizing the unbroken mantra of Silent-Love that's always, already here. Feel It, feel It, feel It, or hear It, hear It, hear It . . . hold on to the path you're on because it is your destiny and is leading you to your destiny. You've made it, and you'll make it.

"What's the most powerful Name of God or mantra?" That's a popular Google search. I contributed to that search in years past. As Krishna Das would say to me, "the most powerful one is the one you chant." So, whether you're chanting "Jesus," or "Allah," or "Maa," or "Rama," or "Krishna," it doesn't matter because all the names are just representative of Love, of this Presence that you are. The Indian saint and teacher, Anandamayi Ma, whose name means "bliss-filled mother," likened the Names to ice figures, noting that when the seeming forms melt, they're the same substance, the same essence—water. And so it doesn't matter which form is most appealing to you. It's not the Name that matters. It's the Love that counts. So, when I'd do my mantra Japa (repetition of a Divine Name of God) practice in the morning, I'd hear, I'd listen to the sound of the Name that came, whether I was saying It aloud (Upanshu Japa), which I did sometimes, like just a whisper, or internally (Manasik Japa—considered the most powerful and also the most challenging to execute of all Japa styles). But I'd say It to Love. I'd hear It in Love. Love is hearing and Love is chanting. Love is what the Name was guiding me to, holding and dissolving me in.

When I'm chanting "Ram" I'm chanting "Love," or "I,"; I'm repeating my own real name over and over again, holding my attention on what I am beyond the appearance of the body for seemingly longer and longer periods of time. Every time I say "Ram," I'm beyond the body. Every time I say "Ram," I'm beyond the body. Every time I say "Ram," the world is seen as a dream. Every time I say "Ram," I know only Love is here.

And during the day, when I wasn't sitting formally with It, or walking formally with It (Love steps) in the foreground, even to this day, I listen to it in the background. I listen to Kirtan music (devotional Hindu music), and I sing along to the Names. I prefer Sanskrit (over English) because the sounds have been practiced by countless other selves for eons and the power is palpable. The Bliss is easy. It's joyful. Music is my life, so it's fun for me, and it would give my mind something else to do. Instead of running the same stuff, those same worries, the same concerns, the same hopes, instead of hearing that, I'd be full of something else, of that one chant, that one mantra, that one thought, this one Love.

And since this world is a projection of what's going on within you, if all that old stuff is replaced, and you've got just this Love inside, what's seemingly projected now? God, Love, This. Peace is what you begin seeing all around you. Initially you sit with it for a period of time every day— five minutes at first beginning this week, working up to an hour). But the true goal is to keep the mantra going all day, every day. It should be the first thing that comes into your conscious awareness when you wake up in the morning, and the last thing you're hearing before you go to sleep at night, hearing your mind repeating that chosen name for you. It should be the last thing you hear at night, the last thing you're thinking at night, the first thing you're thinking in the morning.

Every night before you fall asleep, set an intention to wake up the next morning to Truth . . . to wake up as Love . . . to wake up reciting your mantra . . . to wake up FEELING your mantra . . . feeling Love, smiling, breathing consciously. Then, like we always do, make it a game to stay aware of your mantra (of Love), all the way to the bathroom, all the way to the kitchen, all the way to your office, etc. Keep remembering Love until you realize that you are Love. Everything else is imagination.

And during the day, whenever you find yourself concerned, when you find yourself worried, upset, scared, it's only because you forgot the mantra. You forgot to chant. You forgot your Japa practice. And so you let go of whatever it is that you're thinking about, and you begin to hear, you begin to notice the sound of God's name in you again. And you stay with it. And then thoughts come, and you are paying attention to those thoughts, about what you need to do, or what you didn't do, or what might happen if you don't do. And then you go right back to your mantra, go right back to the name of God. And it gets easier and easier to let go. Krishna Das says, "It's like you're offering everything to that Japa practice," to your mantra. Every thought that comes, you let it go, and you return to your practice. All day, every day.

*I highly recommend Krishna Das's book **Chants of a Lifetime**, as well as **The Way of a Pilgrim**, written by an anonymous Russian monk in the 1800s. If you were raised or are presently Christian, if you lean Christian, and you want to learn how to keep up this ceaseless prayer of the heart, constantly repeating God's name, that's a great book. The chant in that book is, "Lord Jesus, have mercy on me, a sinner." And I did that one for a while too, the shortened version "Lord Jesus, have mercy on me," or simply, "Jesus, have mercy. Christ have mercy." Your mantra may be "Thank you, Jesus." Say that excitedly inside, feeling the joy it stirs, and BE the eternal Son rise! Be(come) Gratitude. If you choose a Christ-based mantra such as one of these, load up the spontaneous worship song by Victor Thompson, "You Are Lifted," and keep it on repeat in the background. It will carry "you" and all of your doubts away. Only Trust will remain.*

In early November 2020, I started working with the Be Here Now Network. Raghu, the CEO, sent me a small mala (string of prayer beads similar to the Catholic rosary, which I collect—I have more than I care to share; two may or may not be in transit as the time of this writing!). It arrived late—weeks after he told me he dropped it in the mail. The envelope was dirty and ripped but the simple wooden mala was inside with a red tassel, and a bit of darker red string wrapped around the base of the tassel. I remember emailing to thank him for it, and asking about its significance, especially the significance of the bit of darker red string. As I awaited his response (which never came via email), I immediately took up the chanting of "Ram" again. I hadn't chanted Ram since my re-reading of *Be Here Now* in 2018 (and prior to that, 2013). I'd chant "Ram" and sing "Sri Ram Jai Ram Jai Jai Ram" all day in Bliss. I would do Love Steps to my favorite versions on Apple Music. But other practices came and went and "Ram" was forgotten, until It showed back up for GoOD.

"I came back from India, chanting the mantra that my Guru was constantly repeating, 'RAM, RAM, RAM, RAM, RAM, RAM, RAM . . .' *Rama* (rhymes with *mama*) or Ram (rhymes with *mom*) is another name for God, or consciousness, or oneness, or love. Rama is the devoted husband of Sita, and the divine masculine form of God. Ram in the spiritual classic the *Ramayana* represents the forces of consciousness and love. He's the perfect balance of devotion, compassion, wisdom and power. Ram is the essence of who you are when you realize your true self."

RAM DASS

"Maharajji was a Ram transmitter. He sounded like a siren. 'Ramramramramramramramramramram!' One of the attainments of great saints is that they become transmitting stations. They go 'on the air' a cosmic channel. Maharaji was broadcasting blessings every moment of the day."

BHAGAVAN DAS

You hear Ram when you're being Ram. You feel Love when you're being Love.

I was a Ram machine during all of 2020—every waking moment. It took over my life. As often as I could, I had the beads going, and when I needed my hands for other things, my mind became the mala, my tongue, I'd hear the mantra going inside. I would read about the Name of Ram constantly (which can also mean Light, or all-pervading Bliss, or Exalted, in addition to the Hindu God ([and King]) Ramachandra from the epic *Ramayana*), to keep myself motivated in the practice, and I came to feel that I had somehow been initiated into the chanting of it. One day while reading a book about Neem Karoli Baba, a great Indian saint who left the body in 1973, I came across a passage about how Ram Dass learned to make malas while in India and would tie a string from Neem Karoli Baba's blanket around each one to bless it. In that moment I knew what I'd been holding in my hand. I later confirmed it with Raghu at the Ram Dass Retreat in Maui (in December 2021). He had sent me my turning-point practice.

"The more I chanted, the more I could chant."

_____

UNKNOWN

The more I chant, the more I Love!

"Ram is the supreme vibration of the Universe."

_____

UNKNOWN

"Bring your mind to one point and wait for grace."

_____

MAHARAJJI TO RAM DASS

If you're having a difficult time listening for the Silence, or listening for the feeling of Love, if that's a little too slippery for you still, and that is okay if it is, mantra is a very effective practice. It's a very ancient practice that every religion has used, is using. Use it. It works. It works, it works. Your mind will tell you that it is useless and you should be doing something else, you have things to think about. Go back, let it go, and then go back to the mantra.

Let it go, go back to the mantra—a mantra in and of itself!

If you want some bonus points, what's even more powerful to recognize is that you're not the chanter, you're not the one reciting the mantra, you're not repeating the mantra, you're just listening to it arise. You're the space, the loving space, the awareness that the chanting is happening within. And so from this perspective, it's much easier to recognize that the mantra is always going. Ram Dass would always say that there's a place inside of him, in his heart, where this mantra goes all the time, like the place in the wall where the candle is lit and that flame is not flickering. That mantra is always going on inside, and it's just a matter of turning within and listening for that. And that means that even when you're in the shower, when you're driving, when you're loading the dishwasher, when you're on the phone, when you're preparing a meal, when you're watching TV, the mantra is going, it's going. And you just have to listen for it inside.

And you'll recognize that when you're upset, or when you're angry, or when you're frustrated, you're not upset, angry, or frustrated, you've just forgotten to listen for the sound of your mantra inside. In that moment, you drop whatever thought stream is there, and you return to listening for the mantra, hearing the name of God. He said if someone was to ask you what you were doing while driving a car, but you were consciously chanting the mantra, you'd reply, "Chanting," because the driving is secondary! You dissolve everything in the divine name. And as Neem Karoli Baba said, "Everything is achieved. Everything is achieved."

I chant knowing the Name is God; It's Love's sonic form, Its sound body, Its present incarnation. I remember what Shiva says to His consort, Uma, in the great Hindu epic *Ramacharitmanas*: "It's all illusion except the Name of the Lord," and I as I hear the chant and look around, it's like I'm knowing, by feeling, Only Love is here, Only God is here, Only Ram is here, Only Light is here. Chanting the name of God is holding your attention on the Word while the world is appearing. It's helping you abide as Love, as the Real, while the false is appearing. It makes everything transparent, less serious, more playful. It turns everything back into Love, even you.

These days, there's just Silence, here. **Nothing needs to be repeated but this Silence. You could say that Loving Silence is my mantra. I Am the mantra. The one who thought she needed to chant to change, dissolves.**

"You must remember that the Name represents God within you. So you repeat any Name you hold dear and fill yourself with Divine ecstasy. This is the easiest and best method by which you can purify yourself. Think of God and you become the image of God. Take the holy Name and you become holy."

SWAMI RAMDAS

"By the power of the Name of God, one shall come to know what one does not know. One shall see what cannot be seen. One will be able to speak what cannot be spoken. One shall meet what cannot be ordinarily met. Incalculable will be the gain of uttering the Name."

TUKARAM

"Gazing upon this world, you are fooled. It is not worth even half a shell. Only the name of the Lord of the Universe is permanent."

SRI GURU GRANTH SAHIB

"After no great lapse of time I had the feeling that the prayer had, so to speak, by its own action passed from my lips to my heart. Further there came into my heart gracious warmth. None of these things made me feel at all cast down. It was as though they happened to someone else and I merely watched them. The Prayer brought sweetness into my heart, and made me unaware, so to speak, of everything else."

THE WAY OF A PILGRIM

The Transforming Power of Now

The "waiting."
Are you filling this gap,
or FEELING It?
Right behind that filler-thought, "But nothing is happening,"
is the Feeling, the Love that Is.
The one who is waiting is not you.
The one who is growing impatient is not you.
The one who thinks every possibility is closed is not you.
The one who keeps finding and losing Faith is not you.
You're not waiting.
You're Loving.
And Love changes everything.

THE QUOTE

"When you rest in quietness, and your image of yourself fades, and
your image of the world fades, and your ideas of others fade, what's
left? A brightness, a radiant emptiness that is simply what you are."

———————

ATTRIBUTED TO ADYASHANTI

THE PRACTICE

Catch yourself when you're aware of thoughts that sound like "Things will be better tomorrow," or "I'll be good after today . . . let me just get through today." That's the same as saying, "I'm not good now . . . I can't feel good, I can't feel the presence of Love, until tomorrow, until later." And you know that's not true: you can only be aware of and AS God now.

When you become aware of thoughts like this, especially on days like these, trying to get to your weekend, or to your next vacation, stop. Catch yourself breathing. Feel for your heartbeat. Feel for God where you are, and watch your world take on Love's image. Don't put off your felt-oneness with Love another second. There is no other second. There is no "tomorrow." When it seems to arrive, it'll be "now," too. Feeling GoOD now ensures that your future "nows" will be Love. Love you can see.

"I've just got to get through today,
then I'll be good.
I've just got to get through this workday, this day.
Things will be better tomorrow."
Does that sound like you?
I think it sounds like all of us.

You are growing in awareness of your thoughts, of your familiar thinking patterns, and while this one doesn't seem unhelpful on the surface, it is, because in declaring that you'll be good after today, or that things will be better tomorrow, you are declaring that God will be better tomorrow, when God is already being God fully, right now. God is always being God. Just like the sun is always being the sun; it's always giving fully. It's just a matter of whether we're standing out in it, feeling its warmth, its presence. With God, Love, you have to recognize that it's in you, and that you're in It. It's taken on your shape while remaining shapeless. Feel this.

"I am ever present to those who have realized me in every creature. Seeing all life as my manifestation, they are never separated from me. They worship me in the hearts of all, and all their actions proceed from me. Wherever they may live, they abide in me."

BHAGAVAD GITA, 6:30-31

"Abide in me as I abide in you. Just as the branch cannot bear fruit by itself unless it abides in the vine, neither can you unless you abide in me. I am the vine, you are the branches. Those who abide in me and I in them bear much fruit, because apart from me you can do nothing."

JESUS (JOHN 15:4-5, NRSV-CE)

So when you say, "I can't feel good until today is over," or "I won't feel good/God until after this test, or I get back those results from the doctor, or until after this week, next month," what happens after this week, after this month? Whatever the issue is that you were deeming more important than your conscious recognition of Love, something else comes up to take its place. A new issue appears. "It's always something," you say. And then you put off the recognition of your Self again. You put off your practice. You put off meditation until after you get that text back, that reply you've been waiting for. *If I can just get through this, then I'll allow myself to feel good, to feel God.*

When you notice thoughts like that, recognize that they are a trick your mind is playing, and immediately listen for Silence, or for your mantra, or for felt-Love, and allow that Love to dissolve the belief that you can't feel God now, that you can't feel good now, that you can only feel

It after. Even if you're at the grocery store and there's a long line and you're in that line but you want to be home, cooking already, eating already—and you're feeling that familiar, anxious energy, notice it and then notice your shoulders and stomach relaxing into the moment fully. Notice your breath calming down into the moment. You're in line and you could not be anywhere else in that moment. That is your full existence. That is your full life right there in that line. Right there in that line, you wake up in that line, in that grocery store, and all of a sudden you are the grocery store, you are the line and everyone in it.

You feel good. You feel God. Everywhere you look, you feel God. You see God. You know God. And then you're not waiting anymore. You're no longer waiting for later. You are no longer waiting until you get home to feel good. You feel God now.

Just like I want you to feel your heart beating now.

Feel for it.

Listen for it.

Notice your breathing.

Relax your shoulders.

Bow your head gently and fold your hands in front of you.

It's as if you're praying to this Love.

"I'm sorry I forget You. I'm sorry I make things more important than You, situations, people, more important than You, that I put things before You when You're the only thing. When You create all the things, You are all the things, and I'm so thankful that I'm remembering that and I'm remembering You, and I'm feeling You more and more in every moment, as the moment itself.

"Throughout the day, when I remember You, I'm so happy and so thankful that I found You, that You chose me to remember You, and I'm trying to remember You, but it's hard. But this day, this morning, I will

recognize that I don't have to wait until office hours are over to feel You. I don't have to wait until happy hour to feel You. I don't have to wait until later to feel You. I can feel You only now, and now I feel You and I sway in You and I smile in You. And the Love and gratitude I feel for You in this moment is actually Your Love, Your Love flowing through me. There's only Your Love, and I've been trying to claim It as my own. I've been dividing Your Love and giving It only to certain people, feeling It only in certain places. And I'm not chopping up Your Love anymore. I'm not dividing It up and divvying It out. I'm just letting that Love flow through this vessel and out into the world. Like the sun shining, your Love is loving. It's not loving more tomorrow or later. It's not loving more next week. It's loving fully now, and as long as I feel it fully now, I have harmony now. I have abundance now. Things are perfect now. I can't see the perfection with my human eyes, but I can feel it. I can feel You and know that you are perfect. This Love is perfect now. And as long as I stay aware of that perfection, even as I walk through this imperfect world, I'll begin to see the forms that take on the image of that perfection. I'll begin to see You everywhere. Thank you for this truth. Thank you for this life. Thank you for Love. I Love you."

This is Your mind on God.
This is your life on Love.
Where every thorn becomes a rose, and every thought becomes GoOD.
You think about God all day, the way you used to think about your problems all day. You feel GoOD all day no matter what comes, by intending, "I'm feeling GoOD anyway."
And you smile.
And the world smiles.
Because God is.
You are.

Remain Happy
Twenty-Four Hours a Day

Even if the world is not smiling back at you yet,
you FEEL its smile,
you FEEL the changes beneath the surface,
you FEEL the GoOD behind the scene,
pervading the scene,
appearing AS the scene.
You know the Secret.
You're in on the Secret,
You ARE the Secret,
and that's why you smile.
Persisting in this Love,
swaying,
looking, and not letting the appearance of the world make you
forget to feel Love.
That's the real change.
And only from here do you see the "outer" one.

THE QUOTES

"Whenever you are sitting and you have nothing to do, just relax
your lower jaw and open the mouth just slightly. Start breathing

from the mouth but not deeply. Just let the body breathe so it will be shallow. . . . And when you feel that the breathing has become very shallow and the mouth is open and your jaw is relaxed, your whole body will feel very relaxed.

"In that moment, start feeling a smile—not on the face but all over your inner being. . . . It is not a smile that comes on the lips—it is an existential smile that spreads just inside. . . .

"No need to smile with the lips on the face but just as if you are smiling from the belly; the belly is smiling. And it is a smile, not a laughter, so it is very very soft, delicate, fragile—like a small rose flower opening in the belly and the fragrance spreading all over the body.

"Once you have known what this smile is you can remain happy for twenty-four hours. And whenever you feel that you are missing that happiness, just close your eyes and catch hold of that smile again and it will be there. . . . It is always there."

―――――――

OSHO, *THE ORANGE BOOK*

"Smiling is one of the highest forms of meditation."

―――――――

ATTRIBUTED TO AMMA

THE PRACTICE

Just take a little moment,
eyes open,
and breathe into your heart.
Pretend your heart itself is breathing.
Just take little,
short,

shallow,
open-mouth breaths
in and out of your heart.
Try it right now.
Feel that energy?!
Let that smile grow from the inside.
Stay with the smile.
Live today, this week, as that smile.
And like you already know,
every time you notice that you've forgotten,
you can close your eyes for a couple of seconds
(like pressing a Reset button)
and come right back to It.
Take those breaths,
smile from the inside out,
and you're back on the Throne!

BONUS PRACTICE

Watch yourself practicing the short, shallow, open-mouth breaths. Be the Loving space for the breathing and the smiling to happen in, rather than being the breather or the smiler. Be the formless, impersonal, boundless, undivided, invisible Love instead of the "practitioner."

I used to meditate every day for three hours. This went on between 2012 and 2015. It felt very necessary during that time. And when I did not get the opportunity to meditate, I was not a very nice person. That was the problem. I thought I was a person that needed meditation—not realizing meditation is something that is happening, that begins, right where you appear to be. Now my life has become meditation. I'm meditating right now. I'm always meditating, whether I'm writing, driving, talking with someone, walking to the beach, loading the dishwasher. All of it's meditation now. But in the beginning, when this practice took hold of me, when this journey launched itself, meditation felt like a part of my life that was very separate from the rest of my life. Like if I was working, I could not be meditating. Because for me, meditating was, at that time, lying on my back in corpse pose, hands to my side, relaxed upward, and I would just be there like that until I wasn't there as Nikki, until there was just this Love. No body, no mind, just a Silence, a very Aware Presence. However, the moment I knew I was aware without thoughts, I was back, baby! Spiritual ego on 100!

The purpose of meditation isn't to still the mind but to encounter God. The mind is then stilled in the presence of God's Love.

It would take about 15-20 minutes. On a rough day, maybe 30 minutes, for me to become aware of a quiet Peace. I'd begin seeing through the thoughts, over their shoulders, and to the Bliss that was between, underneath, and pervading them. But it felt like it would take at least 20-30 minutes of formal meditation, lying down, eyes closed, quiet, private space, no noise, to arrive at this "state."

I remember sitting on the couch one day in our loft in Washington, DC, when I recognized that when I was aware of Love, by the time I started noticing Love in my formal meditation sessions, my mouth was open a little and my breathing was barely perceptible. A very shallow chest breath that was barely happening. Breathing was barely happening when I was in that deeper state of meditation. And I remember sitting on that couch and trying that style of breath and being elated that it seemed to connect me to, or turn me toward, the Love that before I'd thought I could connect to only after allowing thoughts to "hush."

And so I began practicing that. I began using it. And I made a note in my phone titled "How to Shift Right Quick." The instructions read, "Short, quick breaths, breathe into your heart and smile." But I never shared this note with anyone because I thought it was very personal to me and my experiences with meditating and connecting to this Love.

Fast-forward to 2016: I came across a tremendous work called *The Orange Book* by Osho, which is full of practices, and this was one of them. The practice that I had written in my phone years before, that I thought was personal to me, that would make sense only to me, he had arrived at, too. And all of his teachings and practices were inspired by ancient sutras and the Vedas. So this is something that humans have been practicing forever.

I remember being so excited when I read those words for the first time. "It's not just me. This is a thing." My mouth would be so dry after my meditations because it would be open and those little short, shallow breaths were happening. And so, re-creating that in my waking moments during the day, I found that it works. It worked. I don't have to do it anymore. And once you start practicing it (I trust it worked for you now) regularly, you won't have to do it for too long before you're able to just turn right to the Love.

So this week, wherever you find that body, just take a little moment, eyes open, and breathe into your heart. Short, shallow breaths. People won't even notice. Don't even worry about them. Remember, it's just You anyway.

> "Is it just me, or is it just me?"
>
> ———
>
> **UNKNOWN**

So don't worry about the seeming others, and just breathe into your heart. Short, shallow, open mouth breaths. Do it right now. Feel that smile grow. Stay with the smile. Live every day as that smile. And as Osho said, every time you notice you've forgotten, you can close your eyes for a couple of seconds, like pressing a reset button, and come right back to it. Take those breaths. You're back. On your Throne.

I Love You.

Let It surface—
your Smile,
the Silence,
(t)His Love,
the Breakthrough.
They're all Here.
They're all One.
They're all You.
Let It surface.

"Observing the natural breath is a universal practice. Breath is breath, not a Hindu breath, a Muslim breath or a Christian breath."

———————

ACARIYA S. N. GOENKA

We Can't Afford to Stop Feeling Love

When that body slouches,
it's like it's slouching into forgetfulness.
It's slouching into worry.
It's slouching into overthinking.
Sit back up straight,
like you're on your Throne,
and be Greatness.
In this posture, that body is like an antenna,
receiving, remembering Greatness,
remembering its
Divine Essence,
remembering Truth.
Remembering that everything it encounters is also Greatness,
is one with Greatness.
That there is nothing but Greatness.
Only Love exists.

THE QUOTES

"Love, like life, flows
through the heart.

Feel the thrill of the flow
and say nothing."

OFTEN ATTRIBUTED TO RUMI

"The spine is the highway to the Infinite. Your own body is
the temple of God. It is within your own self that God must be
realized. Whatever places of pilgrimage you visit outwardly,
and whatever outward rituals you perform, the ultimate
'pilgrimage' must be within."

PARAMHANSA YOGANANDA

THE PRACTICE

Say less. Feel more.

Do what you have to do, today, this week, but don't stop feeling the
Flow. This Flow is the presence of change. It's the presence of God. It's
the presence of your miracle. It's the presence and evidence of your
new life. Your true life. You are reborn of the Spirit.

> "Don't go with the flow. Be the flow."
>
> ATTRIBUTED TO SHAMS TABRIZI

I trust that it's all good, all God, where you are.
But if it feels heavy right now,
if it feels limiting,
if it feels like you need change,
let that change Flow in and out of you right now.

Change won't come tomorrow
or next year
or in five years
if you don't allow yourself to feel the Flow of change now.

Repeat these words with feeling, aloud or silently, with me:

Love is flowing through me. Love is flowing through my body. Love is flowing through my mind. Love is flowing through my heart. Love is flowing through my life. This flow of love is healing my life. It's changing my life. As I feel this Flow now, everything is new. Everything is changing. Nothing is the same. Love is my life. Love is Me.

Smile, sway, and feel those words.

Stay with one line if you need to until you feel it,
until it lights you up.
Love is my life.
Love is all I see.
Love is all I hear.
Love is all I experience.
And when I am experiencing something that is not Love,
I know I'm perceiving wrongly.
And I close my eyes for a moment and I feel for the Flow behind it,
and I know that only that Flow is there,
only this Flow is real.
And the conscious presence of the Flow is the change,
is the Truth.
I can feel the change
I can't see the change,
but I can feel the change.
I can't stop feeling the change anymore.
I can't afford to stop feeling the change.

And when I open my eyes again,
even if I still see that thing that is not a reflection of Love,
it has changed.
"My enemy said to me, 'Love your enemy.' And I obeyed him
and loved myself." —Khalil Gibran
Keep turning back,
keep getting back within yourself,
feeling the flow and letting that flow out into the world,
to change the world.
It starts within.
It starts with you.
It starts now.
This is your new life.
Say less today, feel more.

The feeling of Flow is the first sign you'll get that your new life
has arrived.

Don't gossip today. Don't make random phone calls when you're bored today. Don't answer that call you don't want to answer today. Idle chatter, none of that today, just this. Do what you have to do today, but feel the Flow while you do it. Set an alarm, write on sticky notes around the house, put in this work of feeling the Flow consciously until it becomes effortless, until only the Flow is, until you're being the Source of the Flow.

> "Straight body, straight breath, straight attention, straight awareness of Consciousness (remembrance of God)."
>
> ———
>
> **GANESH BABA**

This Flow is the presence of every change you've been seeking. This Flow is the presence of God. It's the awareness that you're in the Kingdom, that you are the Kingdom, the Self is the Kingdom. And like it says in the Gospel of Thomas, it's spread out all over the Earth and you just can't see it (see Week 45). It's here in place of Earth, and while you can't see It yet, you can feel It. And the more you feel It, the more you'll see It. In everyone, in everything, you'll feel God where people appear to be; you'll feel God where you appear to be. You'll feel the Flow where your life appears to be, and then you'll see the Flow where your life appears to be.

I love you.

There is nowhere where God is not,
where Joy is not,
where Abundance is not.
You just have to know where to look,
how to look,
how to shift.
And as you shift, the world shifts.
Everything is changing, thanks to you.
Thank YOU.
Keep going.

The Key to Feeling Love All the Time

Feeling the breeze, think, "God is breathing on me."

Feeling the sun, think, "God is shining on me."

Feeling the water, think, "God is cleansing me."

Feeling the Love, think, "God is blessing me."

Use every moment of every day for remembrance of God,

and you'll come to see that it's actually Her remembering you.

THE QUOTE

"Everything is impermanent except the love of God."

—————

NEEM KAROLI BABA

THE PRACTICE

Find the Easter egg in every moment—find the Love behind every thought, person, place, thing, and seeming moment. Find Love in every room you find yourself in. It may start as simply finding your smile, your breath, or your heartbeat in every room.

Find Love in every moment.
No matter what fleeting moment you find that body in,
feel for the Love,
the permanence,
that is behind and beyond it.
Feel Love at the store,
at the office,
at home,
in that one place you've never been able to find It before.
Stay with this Love and know that nothing external is causing It.
It just is,
and you are blessed in this life to be able to be consciously aware of
It.
To be in alignment with It.
To be It appearing as you.
When you live as It,
It becomes everything that is needed.
Trust It.

I like to imagine that in these moments that we share together, you are sipping coffee, or having your tea, and looking out at the new day, while letting not just my words but what I'm actually trying to give, this Love, soak into your being.

That's kinda what It's like. This Love. That first sip of cappuccino in the morning, or that first bit of dessert after dinner when you're looking for something sweet. Or if you've ordered some food and it's been an hour, and you're starving and it finally arrives and they leave it on the doorstep, and you run outside looking a mess, and you grab it, and you bring it back in and you load up Netflix, and then that first bite of food. That feeling—you think it comes from the experience, that the first sip of coffee or these words made you say, "Ahhhhh, yes." No. That's how you feel when you don't want anything, when the desire has subsided.

Because now you have it. You have the thing that you wanted. You have the coffee, you have the tea, you have the first bite of food, you have the new inspiring words, whatever it is. The mind shut up because it didn't need anything in that moment. And in that quiet, you were aware of the fullness of your Self. Or, even better stated, the fullness of your Self was aware of Itself. And It feels like Love, It feels like joy, It feels like a relief, It feels like Peace when It turns back on Itself. That's True Feeling. That's Home Base. Everything else is added on top.

And so our entire purpose together every morning is for you to recognize that you don't need anything to get you there, because you are (t)Here-ness, you are That. It's not really an experience. It's always here, not even under the surface but buried deep. When you're having the thought that you want coffee, or that you need tea, or you need something sweet, that thought is sitting right (t)here in that fulfillment, in this Love you are, as that Peace. You are giving your attention to the desire, to the thought, instead of to the Love. If you can, just one time, in the midst of a desire, like when it comes up—"Oh my goodness, I would love some chocolate right now"—recognize that thought as a thought and then immediately use the thought itself to become aware of the Love that it came from, that it was born of. Just turn right back, turn right back to the Love. You'll be like "Damn, Nikki's right. It's here. It's always here."

You might still get your chocolate, and you'll still enjoy it, but now you know that you are never not in Love. You are never not Love. You don't have to wait on the chocolate to feel your Love, to be yourself, to be Love. You just have to recognize It. Just hold that thread through every moment. Hold that thread while you're having the desires. Hold the thread of Silence. Hold the thread of Truth, of felt-Love, no matter what moment you find that body in.

Your breakthrough is here.
But first you must break through and feel Love.
You must focus on the Love,

on (t)His Light.
No matter what else you're feeling,
no matter what else you're hearing,
no matter what else you're seeing,
you have to feel this Love anyway.
You have to find God.
*Like, **Where's Waldo?***
Every street,
every restaurant,
every seeming moment.
Only you're not looking for that striped shirt;
you're listening for The Feeling.
You listen for the Silence
until the Love rushes in.
And then the search never was.
There's only "Her," again.
Every time you hear the Silence,
even just a little bit,
(t)here's only Love again.

I like to think of it as an Easter egg hunt, every moment that I'm in. For example, right now, I'm about to go to the beach. It's very easy to get distracted at the beach because there's so much to see. Sometimes I can't decide whether to read, or to people watch, or to get some fries. And oh, let me make sure my face is covered. All of these things are happening, but it's a game for me, and it's automatic now to recognize, "Oh, the Love is here." Or if you're at a restaurant, and you're distracted trying to figure out what to order, and you're having small talk with the waiter, and the Grace arises inside: "Oh, the Love is here, too." You shift from being a polite and engaging human to Spirit. You become an image of God.

Or if you're walking down the street and you're surrounded by "strangers" (more of your Self, other waves in the ocean, other fingers on the hand), and you just take a moment to stop being so self-conscious, little-self-conscious, conscious of your little self, of your mask, of your ego, and "Oh, the Love is here, too." If you are a socially awkward person like me, if you're socially anxious, this is the cure-all for that. Because you move from being aware of your little self to being aware of Self. And in that, there's true confidence, real power. Not power over someone or something, because there is nothing else. Just this one power of Love that you are.

This Love is not something you have to pray to, or beg something from, or please by being "good." It is not a power you have to overpower. The moment you know It's here (as your sense of being alive, here, reading or listening to these words . . . the Awareness that hears you internally saying the words you're seeing) and that you're It, It's working on your seeming behalf.

There is no self-consciousness in that; it's just Bliss. And It spills over into the world and into your interactions. You find yourself wanting to talk to people, wanting to be around people, and then, at times, wanting to retreat and rejuvenate yourself and sit in the presence of This alone. You do that, and while you're sitting, you recognize, "Ahhh, here's the Love. I'm practicing being this Love." It's easy to practice when you're alone, and then, when you're out in the world, you can be that Love.

All this week, I want you to find your Easter eggs, whether you're at the office or at home. Find that Love, and then know that It didn't come from anything in the environment. It's not coming from anything external. This Love is uncaused. Nothing is generating It. It just is. The mind likes to say something like "Oh, well, I feel like this because this coffee is on point this morning." Or "I feel like this because of that email" or "because of that sweet text message from my significant other" or "because of this" or "because of that." But no, in that moment, you just became aware of your Self. That's it. It's that simple. The end.

And so, practice remembering that it's fun and beautiful to pretend that there are others and that they can make you feel a certain way. But we're taking our power back, not just from the negative situations and circumstances and people but from the seemingly positive ones, too. Because we know how fleeting everything is, and because we know how everything changes. I'm not telling you not to enjoy your coffee, not to enjoy your tea or your new partner. But become consciously aware in those moments of where that Joy actually is. Of where the Love is actually coming from! Sit back on your throne. Don't wander away into the world. Stay on your throne, in the knowledge that Love does not come and go. It's the only thing that's permanent.

Affirm: "I Am" is my Power.
I Am is the only Power.
All I have to do is hear It,
is feel It,
is be It,
and the earth melts (it's seen as not truly real),
and the miracle happens.

Week 23

Looking for Felt-Love—
Not Signs

Look at Me.

Don't think about "that."

Think about Me and I'll give you "that" or something better,

something that keeps you aware of Me,

something that keeps you in tune with Me,

that keeps you practicing Me,

that keeps you sharing Me.

You can trust Me,

"for I know the plans I have for you,

plans to prosper you and not to harm you,

plans to give you hope and a future" (Jeremiah 29:11, NIV).

What I have manifested for you is much more exciting

than what you're trying to manifest,

than what you're looking for signs of.

I Am the sign.

This love you feel is the sign.

The silence you hear,

that's the sign that you're on the right track,

that you're on the path I paved for you before you even appeared here.

You've never strayed from the path.

Everything was a part of this path.

153

THE QUOTE

"As rapidly as we use the forms as which supply appears, the invisible supply will again become manifest, because it is infinite; it is always omnipresent, and the supply itself, which is the Spirit of God in us, will reproduce it. No longer shall we live by bread alone, but by a consciousness of God's presence which requires no words, but rests in God as one."

———————

JOEL GOLDSMITH, *PRACTICING THE PRESENCE*

THE PRACTICE

Look for felt-Love today, not signs. The feeling of Love is the sign.
Stop looking for signs of your good
for evidence of God.
Recognize and feel your fullness.
Relax into your fullness.
Into the felt-being of Love.
Live this week as THAT which you hope to become.
When you are living as THAT,
you don't look for signs!
You are the sign.

Jesus told us to take no thought for what we shall wear or what we shall eat (Matthew 6:25–34, KJV). But we do. You're definitely thinking about yourself, your needs, your lack, all day long, every day (99 percent of your thoughts are about yourself and your family), with your head on a swivel looking for signs. "When is my wealth going to show up?" "When is this solution to my problem going to show up?" "When is this miracle going to happen?" We keep looking for signs. But not this week. We're not looking for signs today. We're not looking for synchronicities today. We're not looking for evidence of our good. We're not looking for evidence of God. Be honest with yourself: right now, are you reading this as the person who wants or needs something or the person who has? The person who is? Those are two completely different states of being, wanting versus having.

Try this: Expand your desire from trying to solve your problem of lack to being the Loving Solution, radiating abundance out to the whole world. Your family and you will be included in that. Expand. Feed everyone. Bless everyone and you'll always be blessed.

And I'm not saying that you have the added things that you're hoping to get out here in the world. What I'm saying you have is this Love. And I assure you that this Love becomes everything you need out (t)here. This love is God, and it fulfills Itself through you and your experience and your existence. That's what we're practicing. We're practicing being; we're practicing having and letting go of that state where we're wanting and lacking and in need and desperate. You can feel the difference there. And there's no effort. There's no step-by-step process that you have to do now for us to practice this state, this true way of being, which is the one of Fullness.

"I depend on no one because God is my sufficiency in all things. You've got to be centered in God. That's your number one priority. That's all you've got to do at all times is be centered in God. And everything must come your way. It's a law. Spirit draws unto Itself. Spirit will employ you because Spirit is you. But if you're not Spirit, or if you disclaim being Spirit or if you act like a human, and not Spirit, how can Spirit serve?"

————

HERB FITCH

You are Fullness. You don't need anything to fill you up. So you can stop waiting and looking for that and recognize your fullness. It's that simple. You don't have to do anything different. You just have to remember, and we remember by feeling. Feel your fullness today. Don't look for signs. Every time you find yourself in that mode where you're on Instagram looking for that little quote that's going to assure you that everything is fine, or you're looking for the time on the clock to be 11:11 or looking for a license plate to give you some assurance, recognize that pattern of behavior. Recognize that when you're doing that, you're not in Faith, you're not in Love. And I'm talking to both of us, not just you. I'm talking to me, too. Recognize that pattern of behavior and immediately use it as a trigger to remind you to relax, to dissolve into this love.

Do that right now. You can do this wherever you are because, again, you don't have to close your eyes. We can meditate twenty-four/seven with our eyes open, knowing the Truth, feeling the Truth. Just let your body go Jell-O,

relax your whole body around that erect spine.
When your body is relaxed,
your mind naturally calms down.
And when your mind calms down,
it's easier to see through to the Love,
to feel through to the Truth.
And when you are in touch with Truth,
that body,
that person,
that ego, manifests purely;
then you can be You—
the highest-embodied version of your Self.

You show up as the best you that you can be in this world, in this dream, in this illusion. But when you're not connected to that, when you're not in contact with this place, with your Self—well, you know how that feels, you know what that looks like; it's not fun.

So this week, we are staying connected. We are feeling our fullness. And because we are full to the brim, we need nothing from anyone. We know that we have everything we need and that it'll show up exactly when we need it. Not a second before. So stop looking for it.

Jesus told us to worship the Father in and as Spirit. All the Father can give us is His Spirit. Not material things. Just Love. Let Love be enough, and watch It take the shape of the added things you were once looking for.

We're going to exist today and be today as that which we have wanted to become.
We're going to recognize that we already always have been that.
Whatever it is that you're waiting for,
whether it's an experience or an accolade,
when you're aware of this Love,
that thing is making its way to you.
It is coming into form.
That or something better.
And you don't have to believe it.
You don't have to hope for it.
You feel it.
You feel It before you see It.
This Feeling is the Sign that It's here. It's just present as the Feeling right now.

Letting Love Change the Channel

> "Problems are the denial of the presence of God."
>
> ———————
>
> **HERB FITCH**

THE QUOTE

"As you progress you become less excited about collecting the melodrama of the daily news; for as you delve within yourself, you want less and less to feed your mind unnecessary images and thoughts that agitate it. You simplify what you talk about, what you watch, and what you read. You find yourself drawn to new kinds of books, perhaps books written by those who speak from the quiet of meditation. They are invaluable in creating space in which your mind can become quiet also. . . .

"One can be a responsible citizen without allowing one's mind to be captured by the media and their need to create news."

———————

RAM DASS, *JOURNEY OF AWAKENING*

THE PRACTICE

Just for now, turn off and away from anxiety-inducing, duality- and dream-confirming content, and turn toward Love.

What you're not going to do this week is watch stuff that makes you feel bad. Just for this moment, just for today, just for part of this week, turn off the news, turn off that one crime show . . . stop scrolling that Instagram account (and the comments!) that gives you anxiety. Sit with a GoOD book. Listen to GoOD music. Write in your journal. Take a walk. Our life stories have plenty of drama to seemingly cause that inner ruckus—we don't need to consume content that generates even more. STOP. Breathe. Smile. Love. I'm with you in this practice.

In 2017, before I was able to experience this Love as being present all the time no matter what, it still felt as if I would go in and out of It. I was still watching a lot of shows, and I grew up loving horror movies, anything scary. Ghosts especially. I never really liked blood and gore and zombie movies. I watched those, too, but I liked psychological thrillers like *The Others* and *The Sixth Sense*. And then I'd be scared for the rest of the night. I grew up that way. It was my favorite thing. And there's still a part of me that I believe would enjoy a horror movie.

But I remember that in 2017, I was watching the intro to the second season of *The Handmaid's Tale* (Hulu), and I'm not going to reveal anything about the show in case you want to watch it, but it was really intense. I had seen the first season, and I loved it. But with that opening scene for the second season, I was in tears before the show even started, and I could feel that familiar way of being Nikki in my chest, and I could feel that unease in the pit of my stomach. And I thought, "What am I doing?! I'm here, in my room, in my bed. I'm comfortable. I'm blessed." I woke up out of the strong negative emotions from the show into the Love I am, remembering that I was already going through my own tough stories, trying to hold Love through my own problems, and I didn't need any added turbulence—more stories on top of my own seeming ones. Even if the storyline was good and entertaining, I had plenty of storyline happening in my real life. "I don't need this," I thought.

And I turned it off. And my mom and my sister, I believe, were watching and they were like, "Did you see episode three or four?" I'm like, "No, I stopped watching it." I haven't seen any further episodes. I don't know what happened. I don't care. There's a part of me that would like to continue to watch those kinds of shows, but I know that I can't, not for the lifestyle and the way that I'm trying to live. I care a lot about what I feed my body. I'm not always perfect with that, but I'm pretty good about it, and I could see that it is just as important to take care of what I feed my mind and my soul and my spirit.

Even though Ram Dass's quote is not about watching scary movies or very dramatic shows that are excellent, very well written, and very well acted, it's the same thing. If you're addicted to those storylines breaking on MSNBC or CNN, and you can feel that energy within you, you know the energy I'm talking about. The energy you feel when your spouse comes in and upsets you, says something to agitate you, or presses that button. The same energy you used to feel, maybe, when you were in school and the teacher put that test on your desk upside down, and it was just about time to flip it over and see what all you didn't know, see what all you had forgotten from your studying. That same feeling that we've been feeling since we can remember, just attaching different stories and causes to it. It's like we're addicted to it.

So we watch things, we consume things, we read things that generate that very familiar way of being ourselves, of this ego. That's how our ego manifests.

Stop.

That's the whole practice.

Do less of that.

You don't have to stop watching the news entirely. I don't watch it. I read a bit of the *New York Times*. I get little newsletters and, of course, follow social media. I see headlines everywhere, and people who are close to me keep me updated because they know that I don't watch TV. I'm not telling you to be that extreme, but I am saying that you should make some little shifts in your life. Just start small. You are already doing that. You're reading this. You may be listening to Love in the morning with me. That's at least five to ten minutes when you're not watching the news or listening to news. That's awesome.

If you are addicted to crime shows, I get it; I used to watch *Snapped* all the time. I saw every episode and started watching *Fatal Attraction*. They're very entertaining, but they would seem to cause that feeling in me. So whatever it is that you're watching or reading that causes that feeling in you, that agitation, that disturbance, that turbulence, cut back on it this week, and just see how you feel. Fill that space with something else. Pick up a book that is spiritual or that is funny. Pick up a new podcast that makes you feel good, that's empowering. Turn on some music from a time in your life where you were super happy and excited, exuberant. Find something else to do with that time and watch how your body responds. Watch how your mind responds. Again, when your body and your mind are more in harmony, it's easier for you to feel and be this Love, the way you can see your reflection in a still lake but not in a choppy one.

It's not that your body has to be feeling good or your mind has to be quiet and calm for you to feel Love. It doesn't matter what that body-mind is doing. It just makes it so much easier when your body and mind are in harmony and not agitated. So stop agitating them. It's really easy to not turn on a scary show. Just stop doing that thing you do that takes you out of Love. Stop watching that thing you watch that pulls you out of your Self. But if you must watch something disturbing, like if your partner or roommate has something on already, challenge your Self by thinking, "Let me see if I can stay aware of Love while I watch this dramatic crime thriller show." Or you can watch yourself watching the show . . . or watch that body watching a screen. Pan out by seeing that you're already panned out. You're already taking in the whole scene, being the whole scene. The whole appearance you take to be your life is just one big screen and you've never been in it, even though you feel that main character energy!

In truth, you can't give up anything until it's time. You become so full of this Love that you stop seeking Love in a glass or in the fridge or in a book, text, or TV show. You finally know It's within, and you sit back and you're Full. I tried to give up alcohol for years. I never was addicted to it or abused it, but I could feel that after even one drink I was unable to remember to remember God. I didn't like that. I continued to drink socially even when I stopped keeping wine in the house, and even the quarterly social outing got to be too much. I didn't give it up; Love just filled me up. I didn't need it anymore. The Love will have that body eating better, working out, speaking out from It, powerfully. Just practice and watch.

Love + Consistency = Miracles

THE QUOTES

"God . . . may I trust that change will come with consistency, however slow the pace may seem."

DAYAL GAURANGA (@DAYAL.GAURANGA ON INSTAGRAM)

"The best service you can do is to keep your thoughts on God. Keep God in mind every minute."

NEEM KAROLI BABA

THE PRACTICE

Before you eat or drink anything, feel for Love. Feel the felt-Presence where you are, or say your mantra or the Lord's Prayer. Use food and drink to turn you around to your Self repeatedly during the day. When you're three or four bites in, or the entire meal is finished, and you've only then remembered, smile and be thankful for Grace. Grace woke you up, and if you keep intending and practicing, it'll keep waking you up, and sooner and sooner each time. Make it a game!

I remember a time when it felt like I had been practicing exactly what I'm sharing with you right now on a very consistent basis, for a very long time. I was reading about it for sure, constantly from morning to night. And it felt as if I was putting what I was reading into practice, but I wasn't seeing many changes, "inner" or "outer," "spiritually" or "materially." And I was really wanting outer change (not realizing yet that they are one—there's no division). I remember taking a step back and making a true assessment of the whole situation. I thought, "How often am I actually in Presence? Like actually feeling God's Love?" And around that time, I heard a talk by Eckhart Tolle during which a member of the audience asked him, "How often are you living in the now or living as the now?" And he actually answered with a number. It wasn't some vague thing that a lot of spiritual teachers say; he said, "I'd say eighty percent of the day I am aware of presence."

I thought, "Well, goodness, if it's just eighty percent for him and he's been at this for a very long time, what's the hope for me? And am I being honest with myself?" And so I decided that, okay, every time I go to eat something or take a drink, anytime I put anything in my mouth, I'm going to become aware of the presence. Because remember, I make everything into a game to make it fun. But this game also showed me how often I was not in Presence. I started in the morning, remembering that every time I picked up a glass of water to sip from, before I took that sip, before the water touched my lips and my tongue, I needed to become aware of this felt-Presence, to become aware of Love. It's kind of like saying grace before your food, but again, it's a felt experience, that God contact.

And at the end of the day, I was shocked by how many times I had forgotten. I more often than not found myself in the middle of my second bite, or on my third gulp of whatever beverage, before I recognized that I had not been Love-Conscious. And so you very quickly come to see that although your mind tells you, "Oh yeah, girl, you're doing great! You are practicing this stuff. You're the best Presence feeler to ever grace this plane!," it's simply not true.

You can't listen to the mind. You can't trust what it is reporting. You have to do your best to practice, and you have to do things like this to keep you aware, to keep you coming back. And so that's this week's practice—becoming aware of this Love; even if you are not very familiar with this Love yet, where you can't just turn to it on a dime, at least become aware of your mantra. A mantra as simple as "Only Love is here." Or remembering, "Thank you, Love, for this water." "Thank you, God, for this cookie." If you can't just turn to Love, pick some words that'll help you get to the Love. And say those words and/or feel that Love before you put the thing in your mouth, before you drink the water, before you have the juice. Make that intention. And then you'll see how frequently during the day you have fallen asleep, that your whole snack is gone. The whole bag of chips is gone before you realize that you forgot. But when you remember you're back on the Throne, you're back. That's Grace. That's like God tapping you on the shoulder. Like, "Hey, hey, remember the intention today?" So it's not that you feel bad about yourself; you feel grateful because it could have been next week before you woke up and remembered this intention! I'm grateful every single time I'm three bites into my meal. I do usually say, "Damn, again?!" but I'm so grateful that I remembered as quickly as I did. But also, it shows you if you're looking around wondering, Where is the change? Where is the change? You're not going to see change unless you're doing something different or, in our case, unless you're being something different.

And we're practicing being Love and we forget because we have practiced being human for so long. But we're turning the tide a bit, little by little every day. And this shows us how much more we have to do, how much more we have to be. And it also just gives us something to come back to throughout the day so that we don't get completely lost. So every single time you're going to eat or drink, you're remembering Love. And that's a lot if you snack as much as I do; I graze all day. So if you're like me and you're a snacker, or if you sip water, you keep your bottle of water by you. That's a lot of little reminders throughout the day to return to Love, to be Love(d), to practice love, to extend Love, to recognize that only Love is here. That this is not water; this is Love. This is not a cookie; this is Love appearing as a cookie.

Try this modified Grace before you eat and drink all week—just remember Love. Feeling Love is the prayer; it is Grace. Remember Love every single time, and it'll show you how much you forget and it'll keep you coming back to what matters, to what's important.

"Suffering is sent to remind you to turn thoughts towards that which is real—to God, who will give you solace."

ATTRIBUTED TO ANANDAMAYI MA

God Doesn't Go Away
When We Are Not Praying

THE QUOTES

"Even though the meditator may leave the meditation, the meditation will not leave the meditator."

—————

DUDJOM RINPOCHE

"Silently intone a word ending in *ah*. Then in the *hh*, effortlessly, the spontaneity. . . ."

"Emphasis should be given to the ending *ah*. Why? Because the moment this sound *ah* is intoned, your breath goes out. You may not have observed it, but now you can observe: whenever your breath goes out you are more silent, and whenever your breath comes in you are more tense."

—————

OSHO, *THE BOOK OF SECRETS*

THE PRACTICE

Extend and feel the "ahhh" sound as you call on Jehovah, Rama, or Issa (Jesus) in your heart.

"God doesn't go away because we are not praying."

This means that just because we forget to feel Love, just because Love seems to be covered up with drama, that doesn't mean It isn't (t)here. When anger comes in the front door and is given our full attention, Love doesn't go out the back door. It's still (t)here. Silently intone the "ah" sound. Inwardly say a name that ends with "ah," like *Issa (Jesus in Arabic), Yeshua (Jesus in Hebrew), Buddha, Rama, Krishna, Mata, Jah, Allah, Shiva, Durga, or Jehovah.*

Coincidence, or nah? Nahhhh, of course! Pick a name of God and repeat it inside, focusing on the relaxation-inducing "ahhhhh" at the end. Recognize that God is easy to feel in the "ah" but that It was there during the inhale, too . . . and between breaths, and before you took your first one. God is, and you are That. Stay aware of this constantly today. Uninterrupted awareness of the presence of God. That's our Work. And our Joy.

You believe you're alone, carrying all of this on your shoulders.
You believe in the world because you forgot the Word.
And when you forget the Word, it's like you forget to exhale.
Focus on the Peace of the exhale with me.
Feel the relaxation of that, how it brings your shoulders down,
how it relaxes your face and your jaw.
The tongue relaxes down from the roof of your mouth.
Your stomach is soft and pooched.
Your legs are relaxed,
and you can even feel that good,
that God, vibration in your feet
that somehow simultaneously grounds you
and keeps you in this Transcendent Awareness,
as this Transcendent Awareness.
Keep exhaling.
Keep relaxing.

Remember this.
Relaxed you is more your Self.
The awareness of this relaxation,
of this God Vibration where you are,
is meditation.
Eyes open or closed, It's still here.
Even though you see the world,
(t)His Vibration is still here.

It's just as loud when your eyes are open as when your eyes are closed.

I want you to stand up and walk around the room you're in. But don't stop feeling This. Don't let go of the thread, this Love.

Hold It as you walk around that room in meandering circles, seeing stuff, hearing stuff, feeling stuff, recognizing that all of that can be happening while you're remembering God, while you're still in meditation, that you can live this life in meditation. You just have to stay alert.

You have to recognize the importance of this, the importance of keeping It in the forefront, in the foreground, recognizing that whenever you think you've lost It, you're just one exhale, one "ah," away from It. And that's not even true. In the beginning, it just seems like that, and that "ah" is a good permission slip to relax back into It. But even the "ah," the remembrance of that and the doing of it, is all happening in the already present Love. You are not turning the Love back on. Everything is happening in the Love, in the "ah," even the forgetting, and the remembering, and the "ah"-ing. The exhaling is happening in this Love. So is the inhaling, and so are the anger and the joy and the wins and the failures.

> "Inhale, and God approaches you. Hold the inhalation and God remains with you. Exhale, and you approach God. Hold the exhalation and surrender to God."
>
> ———
>
> ATTRIBUTED TO TIRUMALAI KRISHNAMACHARYA

Life is happening in This, but only this Love is real. Only this Love is here, and this Love is another name for God. It's another name for You. That's why everyone you meet is your Self, and that's why you treat them the way you want to be treated, because it is You. That's why you feed them. That's why you serve them. That's why you Love them, because it's all You.

> "Carry your meditation as the eternal present, and saturate your everyday life in it."
>
> ———
>
> YOKA-DAISHI

> "For me, prayer is nothing more than a sense of God's presence, an overwhelming awareness of Divine love. This awareness continues uninterrupted, both in prayer times and throughout the day. Why should we see any difference? God doesn't go away because we are not praying. That is why I continue to walk constantly with God, giving God all my strength."
>
> ———
>
> BROTHER LAWRENCE

I Am Risen

You have felt this before.

It's not different from last time.

It's been with you your whole life.

See it.

Be with it.

Breathe through it.

Breathe it out.

Affirm: "I'm out. God's in."

THE QUOTE

"It is the frequency, not the length of time, that makes it natural. That to which you constantly return constitutes your truest self. Frequent occupancy of the feeling of the wish fulfilled is the secret of success."

—————

NEVILLE GODDARD

THE PRACTICE

Breathe through heavy and uncomfortable feelings like they're birthing pains. Feelingly affirm: "'I' in the midst of me is mighty" (Joel Goldsmith's take on Zephaniah 3:17), or "God in the midst of me is mighty"; they have the same meaning.

The neuroscientist Jill Bolte Taylor tells us that an emotion lasts only ninety seconds. And if you can wake up during those ninety seconds and remember,

"I'm not upset.
I'm aware of this upset.
I'm aware of this emotion.
I'm aware of this wave.
Conscious breathing is my anchor . . ."
and just ride it out, just breathe through it,
then that awareness of the breathing, you know it as the Healer,
the awareness of the upset is the healing of the upset.
It's the same awareness of this moment and of that body relaxing.
I remember going through a period when fear would come once a day.

It seemed almost to be predictable, about the same time of day, similar thoughts, same emotion.

One day, I was in the kitchen and I grabbed the counter as if I were having a birthing pain. I just grabbed the counter and I held on, without trying to make it go away, without trying to think my way out of it, without judging myself, without judging the situation, without trying to come up with a solution.

In that moment, I just held on and I could feel my breathing. I listened for the Silence, and in that Silence I remembered, *"God in the midst of me is mighty,"* and I knew that God to be the I Am, the Consciousness that was aware of the fear, that saw it come, the Consciousness that is primary, that must be there first for me even to notice the fear, the Consciousness that began to feel it abating, to feel it lessening in intensity until there was an awareness of being back at zero.

You know how you say you're "feeling like yourself again"? I was feeling like myself again, but more than myself; it was myself mixed with a Peace, a Power, a sureness. But even though I could not yet see a solution, I had one.

You have one right now,
to that problem,
your problem,
you have an answer,
as sure as you have breath flowing in and out of your nose.

The Hindu spiritual teacher Sivananda said, "Every beat that throbs in the heart, every artery that pulsates in the body, every thought that arises in the mind, speaks to you that God is near."

Where the Spirit of the Lord is, there is liberty, there is Peace, and that Peace becomes your answer; it becomes your solution, it becomes the opportunity, the employment; it becomes the cure, the miracle, the promise fulfilled. All you have to remember is to feel that promise, the presence of that promise of Love, while the anger or the fear is there. You don't let the anger or the fear interrupt your communion, interrupt your meeting with God. That is always happening, the meeting with your Self, remembering your Self. All you're doing is staying aware of your Aliveness, your Beingness, which is the Father, the Son, and the Holy Mother in the midst of "you."

Ask yourself, **"Am I aware?"**
The Silence that follows the question is the answer.
You stay with the Silence.
"Is Peace here?"
That's another good question.
"Is Love here, too?
Anger is here;
is Love here, too?"
And you listen.
Even if a "yes" follows the question,
even if a "no" follows the question,
you hear the Silence, too.

The Silence is the Peace,
It is the Love,
It is your True Self,
It is the Presence of God.
We have to keep reminding ourselves that It's here, which is the
same as the feeling "I am here." Affirm that confidently:
"I am here,"
"I am here,"
and now, tell me you're here without telling me you're here.
Feel your hereness,
your silent hereness.
No words,
no thoughts,
no announcement.
Just let the Presence announce itself.

Feel that "I am" is here. Feel that bread, that water, that meat that you have, that the world knows not of. That's your abundance; that's your life. You don't have to worry about tomorrow or next week or next year. You don't have to worry about anything. You just have to be aware of This, and stay aware of This, and Love This. Love your hereness, that Presence, Love It.

When you keep returning here, when you keep remembering what you are, even while what you're not appears to be present—the anger, the fear, the "you," that ego—you operate as if magically. The Hindu spiritual teacher Sadhguru says, "As gravity is active, Grace too is constantly active. It is just that you have to make yourself available to it."

That body is smiling now, and it's swaying gently in this Presence that You are. Its shoulders have come down,

its tension has come down,
and its blood pressure has probably come down, too.
Its thoughts, when they come, will be more positive,
will be more productive, more focused.

Its actions will be more considerate and more powerful, and it'll be better equipped to navigate the emotions (Love appearing as anger, sadness, etc.) that come.

Today and this week, you'll immediately remember who you are, what you are, the "I am" in the midst of that body. That body will begin breathing consciously, and it'll have the thought "This emotion is temporary; it's only going to last about ninety seconds." Just breathe, breathe and feel, and then it feels You. It feels God's Peace; it feels free. The highest truth is that that body can't be free; there's no freedom for it. It doesn't exist. It feels Your freedom, it detects Your freedom. That's why it desires freedom, because what You truly are is free and always has been.

Keep remembering this. I can feel your remembrance. I can feel you waking up out of thought, out of the dream of being that body, out of the nightmare of having those limitations. You're going to wake up out of an emotion today. You're going to remember who you are while the emotion is there, and that'll be the beginning, a new way to live in this world. Rumi said, "Absorbed in this world, you've made it your burden. Rise above this world. There is another vision."

Every time you breathe and feel your way through an emotion, you have risen.

Breathe and feel you have risen,
feel the sun in your heart and know,
"I am risen,"
"'I am' is risen."

"A monk decides to meditate alone for some time. From his monastery, he takes a boat and sets sail in it on the lake. When he reaches the middle of the lake, he moors the boat there. He closes his eyes and starts meditating. After a few hours of undisturbed silence, he suddenly feels a bump of another boat colliding into his own. With his eyes still closed, he senses his anger rising, and by the time he opens his eyes, he is ready to scream at the boatman who dared to disturb his meditation. But when he opens his eyes, he sees that it was in fact an empty boat that had probably got untethered and floated to the middle of the lake. At that moment the monk achieves self-realization and understands that the anger is actually within him. It really just needs the bump of an external object to provoke it out of him. From then on, whenever he came across someone who irritated him or provoked him and made him angry, he reminded himself, "The other person is merely an empty boat. The anger is within me"

N. K. SONDHI AND VIBHA MALHOTRA,
KNOW YOUR WORTH

Remember: The monk's boat is empty, too. In fact, there are no boats, there is no lake. Only Love is here.

The next time anger is felt, experienced in your vessel, in your Emptiness, recognize that you have felt it before. That it's not different from last time or the time before that, or the time before that. That it's been with you your whole life, and at one point you thought it was caused by what your mother did or didn't do, or what your teacher said, or that friend who left, or that one who broke your heart.

Notice that, this feeling, you might not call it anger. You might call it jealousy. You might call it frustration. You might call it annoyance. Whatever name you give it, no matter how mild or intense it appears to be in that moment, this one has always been with you, has been inside you. But you point outside and say, "You are the reason I feel like this." "That is why I'm feeling this way." But this time, like when Jesus said, "Behold, I will do a new thing," you will do a new thing today. You will behold the anger. You will watch and wait, and you will see it go.

The spiritual guru Sri Sri Ravi Shankar likened anger to a little donkey. He said, "It's not a pack of wild horses like it seems to be. It's a little donkey and it comes in one door and goes out the other. If you don't get on it and ride it." He said, "That donkey might create a stir, some dust. It'll kick some dust up, but allow it. Watch it." Watch that anger as if you're watching someone else, as if you're watching someone else's anger, minus the judgment, minus the stories.

You can even empty the anger of the word "anger." Now it's just pure energy, and you know how pure energy feels. Breathe it in and smile, and breathe out the thoughts. Breathe out the labels. Breathe out the anger. Watch it dissipate, that wave of anger, back into the ocean. It was only ever the ocean. It was only ever water. It looked like anger. It felt like anger. You called it anger, just as we call waves waves. But it's just water, empty of labels, empty of thought. You're just this, Silence.

The Indian philosopher and spiritual teacher U. G. Krishnamurti said, "Real silence is explosive. It is not the dead state of mind that spiritual seekers think. . . . This is volcanic in nature. It's bubbling all the time—the energy, the life—that is its quality." This Energy, this pure Energy, this Life, this Love, is your purpose and your fullness. Empty of yourself, you're full of This, and it's This I love.

"Nothing can stop what God is about to do in your life."

_____

NEIL VERMILLION

"Everyone is My body, but they don't hear Me. You do."

_____

LOVE

The Foundation
for All Abundance

THE QUOTE

"From joy I came, for joy I live, in sacred joy I melt."

_____

PARAMHANSA YOGANANDA

THE PRACTICE

Allow Joy to be the foreground of your experience, not the background.

Eat joyfully, drive joyfully, breathe in Joy, walk in Joy. Do everything you normally do but with conscious Joy. Do all of it as if you are existing and moving in and through a Joy bubble . . . feeling this same Joy within and without. The more you remember to feel this all-pervasive Joy, the more your life changes. The instant you feel Joy is the instant the changes begin.

> "Acknowledging the good that is already in your life
> is the foundation for all abundance."
>
> _____
>
> ECKHART TOLLE, *A NEW EARTH*

Make a quick mental list of the good things in your life right now.

Maybe you go to your family, your friends, the people you have been blessed with, the things you have been blessed with, and that's beautiful. If you must focus in this world, that's a much better way to focus: on what you've already been blessed with, on what you have, instead of on what you do not have, what's missing.

The only issue comes when you lose someone, someone who you felt blessed your life. When you lose something, or when something doesn't work out the way you thought it would, the way you needed it to, then you're left sad, grieving, sometimes angry, and frustrated. According to *A Course in Miracles*, these are all calls for Love. They're calls to focus on the good, to focus on God. If we were to reword Tolle's quote—acknowledging *the God that is already in our life* is the foundation for all abundance.

We start this journey by looking around and feeling grateful for all that we've been given, all that we have received, and even for when we are able to give. However, at the next level, while that still happens, while we're still receiving, appreciating, and sharing what we've received, we have to shift our focus, like Douglas Harding and his Headless Way teachings, and turn it back 180 degrees, back onto the One who is doing the seeming receiving and the seeming giving. Who is that one? What is that one?

The author and mindfulness expert Jon Kabat-Zinn said, "Wherever you concentrate, there must be a you to concentrate, and that is what you must concentrate on. That is what you must focus on." Turning your attention around, to focus on the Kingdom within you, to stay aware of God within you, of the good within you. That's the foundation for all Abundance, that's true Gratitude, knowing where everything springs from, what it is born of, knowing that every form, no matter how beautiful, no matter how helpful, is fleeting. It's here today, gone tomorrow. And you'll find no peace until you find this Presence that is not changing, until you find this relaxing that's happening now in those shoulders and that stomach and that face, the smile that's coming to that face, the Joy that's gently bubbling up inside, seemingly prompted by that smile, as if that smile is reminding your cells, your whole being, what it was born to do. You're back on—there's Lightness, there's Joy, there's Love, there's Peace, there's Well-Being. There's Relaxation here, and It is uncaused. You're not creating It, you don't have to maintain It; you just have to get still enough to notice that It's here. That you're here. Not just as the appearance of that body but as the Light that you're feeling, the Light that you're being. Right now you are that Light, appearing as a body, smiling.

And when you remember that, that's focusing on the good, and you don't have to focus on the external objects. You can keep your journal and write down the things you're thankful for every day. That's fine. But at the end of that activity, you must turn within and focus on the Source of everything that you wrote down on that piece of paper. If you wrote down that you're thankful that you got to pay the bills this month, know the true Source of those dollars, the True Employer, the one that has seemed to employ your boss to pay you. And even if your boss was gone and that company was gone, the True Employer would employ another opportunity, another channel for that abundance to reach you, because you're focusing on the real good.

When I focus on the real good, the true good, and moments that are easy, like Sunday morning, this body sways and smiles. It wants to share this Love. That's why I do this, or why It does me. This is a natural unfolding from this Love, every day. And then, when I focus on the good when I turn within to try to feel for God in a busier moment and a more challenging moment like Monday morning, it's not further away, it's not covered up, it's not diminished; and because I practiced on Sunday morning, Monday is easier. It's still right there, right there on the surface. And even though this body is running around getting kids to school, getting back home, sending emails, and running errands, as long as the focus is on the good, life is good. Life is still busy, but it's good because life is God. It's seen as That. You stay in touch with the feeling of Love; that's focusing on the good.

> "The only thing you must remember is how fortunate you are.
> When you forget this you become sad."

———

SRI SRI RAVI SHANKAR

When you forget this Love, you become worried. You become thought full. Full of thoughts. And when you remember Love, you become Silence, minus the word "Silence": just This, just This.

This week, as you sit on the couch, as you sit in the kitchen, as you stand in the bathroom, as you walk down the hall, as you stroll down the street, as you drive your car, as you lie down to rest, no matter what the body is doing, you're focused on the good. You're feeling God on the outside, just walking. Walking's happening, but at the same time, you are in touch with this Joy. It's Joyful walking, it's Joyful driving. It's Joyful sitting. It's Joyful breathing. It's Joyful eating, Joyful planning. We have to plan for tomorrow. There's no Joyful worrying, though. If there's no active planning that can be done for tomorrow, don't just be thinking about what has to happen tomorrow. You drop that and you go back to feeling Him, the One that's going to do the work tomorrow through you. That has never given you any work you cannot do. Everything you do, if you do it for Love, if you do it for God—not for your boss, not for your coworker, not for your wife, not for your husband—if you do it for God, Maharajji said, the work will get done by itself. It feels more effortless.

You work in Joy and it becomes Joyful work. This Joy informs all aspects of your life. It flows through every moment of your life, Joy, and don't stop feeling this Joy today. Every moment you catch yourself not focused here, return here, remember my voice, and return to Joy, return to the smile. Your ability to remember That, to be That, is a miracle, and then your life becomes evidence of that miracle.

Smile, Beam, Trust— Everything Is Right on Schedule

THE QUOTES

"Worrying is like paying a debt you don't owe."

———————

OFTEN ATTRIBUTED TO MARK TWAIN

"If the problem can be solved, why worry?

If the problem cannot be solved, worrying will do you no good."

———————

SHANTIDEVA

"Be empty of worrying. Think of who created thought! Why do you stay in prison when the door is so wide open? Move outside the tangle of fear-thinking. Live in silence. Flow down and down in always widening rings of being."

———————

RUMI

"As I count to three my worries leave me . . . 1, 2, 3."

TANAAZ CHUBB, MY POCKET MANTRAS

THE PRACTICE

Catch yourself mid-worry and smile.
Remember, you're only able to catch yourself mid-worry
because you caught God's Voice . . .
because Grace caught you.
The ability to become Aware,
to become the Witness mid-thought,
mid-worry, IS Grace.
We think we're doing It.
We think we're practicing It.
But It's happening to us.
We're waking up as It.
Smile, Beam, Trust. Everything is right on schedule.
You'll still do the things.
You'll still pay the bills.
But It's Love paying Love.
As long as you have Love,
you'll have Love to pay,
Love to give,
Love to share.
When you forget It, It looks like money you don't have,
like relationships you don't have.
like problems you do have.
If you ARE Love,
you have everything.
And you must rest on that.
Trust in this.

"The more a soul trusts, the more it will receive." —Jesus, in
**Divine Mercy in My Soul: Diary of Saint Maria Faustina
Kowalska**
The quieter you become inside,
letting that tidal wave of Silence hit you,
wash through you,
the more you will receive—
the more comes in on that wave,
the more treasures come in on that wave,
get washed up from the bottom of that sea.

Instead of placing your attention on thoughts, you can place your attention on their Source. Just like right now, you are aware of these words, but you can give attention to the space that they are coming out of, the blank space   between them. You can pay attention to these words and at the same time notice the Stillness, the wordless Space, and know that it is the one that's not changing. These words are changing, that voice inside is changing. The Silence doesn't change.

The thoughts change from worry to hope, back to worry. Worried about tomorrow, about next week, about next month.

Today, every time you catch yourself worrying, get excited. See it as an opportunity to practice. It's come like a pop quiz. And so you catch the worry and you stop in your tracks. Let's say you're preparing lunch and you're at the counter. You're watching those hands, they're going, arranging plates, reaching for the knife, grabbing a tomato, and then the worry comes and you stop everything. Freeze. Suddenly stopping. The body stops. The mind stops—and the subtle thought arises, "As I count to three, my worries leave me. One, two, three," and then linger in that Silence that follows "three," and then wash those hands, get back to cutting that tomato. You'll watch that body eating and you'll notice thoughts again; stop, sandwich half raised to your mouth. And you smile because you caught it. And again you say, "As I count to three, my worries leave me. One, two, three." And stay in that silence after "three" for as long as you can. While that body continues to eat its sandwich.

This mantra comes from Tanaaz Chubb from her book *My Pocket Mantras.*

You're able to catch yourself mid-worry only because you've caught God's voice, because Grace caught you. The ability to become aware mid-thought, mid-worry, is grace. We think we're doing It. It looks like we're doing It. We have to try to practice It and repeat this mantra, but we wouldn't even be able to if we weren't already feeling God sometimes, if God wasn't already waking us up, tapping us on the shoulder. You were having that worry thought, bringing that sandwich up to your mouth, and God tapped you on the shoulder. That Silence tapped you on the shoulder. Remember Me?

"Everything is fine. All is well. You are mine completely, and I'm handling everything." That's what that Silence is saying to you, emanating to you. That's that Love you feel. When I feel this Love, it doesn't matter how scared I was or how worried I was; I know I'm safe. It's like a blanket, like a weighted blanket. And then you put faith in that, and at that moment the mind isn't creating worries. It's not creating problems. The problems are dissolving because the worries have dissolved. And now that Love that's hugging you, that's the world you see. Just as Love replaced worry in your mind, Love will replace the situations in your life, will completely change your world. Don't work harder today or this week. Trust harder. I'm trusting with you right now. I'm still beaming Love to you right now. You have nothing to worry about and everything to celebrate. Smile, beam, and trust. This is God's work, Your work, and God has no worries.

If you have Love, you have everything. You have to rest on that. Rest in this. The seventeenth-century Carmelite monk Brother Lawrence would say he felt as if he was resting on God's breast, on his chest, like God was his mother. How comfortable, how wonderful, that must have felt. That must feel. He didn't get that experience because he was a monk. He got that experience because he practiced just like you're practicing resting in God, on God, as God, trusting. Jesus told the Polish nun and mystic Saint Faustina, "The graces of My Mercy are drawn by means of one vessel only, and that is—trust. The more a soul trusts, the more it will receive." The more you let that tidal wave of Silence hit you, wash through you, the more you will receive, the more comes in on that wave, the more treasures come in on that wave, get washed up from the bottom of that sea.

Week 30

As Your Silence Grows,
Your Success Grows

To make it more specific to your situation,

swap out "success" for "business,"

swap out "success" for "love,"

swap out "success" for "readership,"

swap it out for "audience,"

swap it out for "family."

As my Silence grows, my success grows.

As I grow more and more silent,

I grow more and more in alignment.

I grow more and more in purpose,

in passion.

In Love,

I bloom.

THE QUOTES

"The escape is through the Sound Current."

_____

HAZUR BABA SAWAN SINGH

"Always listen to the inner Sound during meditation every day: If you listen for ten minutes, or five minutes, or four minutes, or two minutes, or even one minute, with love and devotion, millions of sins and obstacles will be removed."

—————

BABA JAIMAL SINGH

THE PRACTICE

Inwardly state, "Lead us not into temptation," defining "temptation" as thoughts of any kind. Become aware of the Sound of Silence—the Divine Sound Stream beyond thought, the mind's original state. Jump into that Stream. Don't get out.

Your Silence isn't dead or boring. It isn't flat. It's rich. It's the sound of Light. Listen as if your right ear were a satellite, and hear what pitch your Silence is in. Listen as It builds. As It sings. As It calls you Home, out from fear, doubt, and lack, which simply means you've been called out of the thinking mind and into the mind that is in Christ Jesus. The Buddha Mind. Only Abundance of Silence, of Divine Sound, of Light and Love, is here, and they're all different facets of the Ever-Shining One that you are.

Make an effort to hear the Silence now, and later you'll
enjoy a pension.
Later, this Silence will just be (t)here without you having
to work for It.
This Love will just flow to you,
to the new you,
to the retired you.
The one who Love is retiring from that unhealthy job,
from that toxic relationship,
or from that version of you that didn't feel confident,
that version of you that didn't feel Go(o)d.

You're retiring from being that one,
and you're stepping into this new life where
all you know is God,
and the things of God,
and the people of God,
and the service of God.
Your whole life is changing.
Right now, as you read these words,
relaxing your shoulders,
feeling GoOD,
you're changing your whole life.
Keep holding God with both hands today,
and know God is holding you, too,
retiring, returning, you to His self.

"Always keep your mind fixed on God. In the beginning you must struggle a little; later on you will enjoy your pension."

SRI RAMAKRISHNA

"Do your work with one hand and hold onto God with the other. When you finish your work, you will hold God with both hands."

ATTRIBUTED TO SRI RAMAKRISHNA

On a silent retreat at the Franciscan Center in Tampa Bay, Florida, I walked the grounds constantly repeating a line from the Lord's Prayer "Lead us not into temptation"—using that as a cue to keep me in the Silence, to stand me still in God. During formal meditation one morning early in the retreat, it dawned that "temptation" means thoughts. Lead me not into more thinking, into more doubting, into less trusting of you, God, into less focus on Love. The whole purpose of our work here is to notice the Silent-Love until the noticer is dissolved. This simple pointer kept me from going down any rabbit holes, even the good ones. It held me in the Peace that Love (Jesus's other name) left us. Defining "temptation" as any thought, even the good ones, will keep you from thinking about any thought that may crop up. But of course I still found a thought to follow—one that questioned God, "What is the key to You? To keeping You, the Awareness, the Love of You here? How can I lock you in my heart, even when I get back out there, when I go back out into the world, into the noise?" And my feet, they kept walking; they took me farther than I had gone on the path previously, and I came upon a park bench. It had something sparkly hanging from its side. It looked very strange from a distance, and to get to it, I had to cross some sand that looked very rocky, very sketchy, like thorns and rocks and jagged shells. And I was barefoot, because I'm often barefoot.

> "What is meant for you, will reach you even if it is beneath two mountains. And what is not meant for you will not reach you even if it's between your two lips."
>
> **ARABIC PROVERB**

I could feel Love inside saying, "You'll be fine. You won't cut your feet." And so I, still very carefully, walked across that patch of rocky sand to get to the bench, to get to that item that had caught my eye. And it was a bracelet, like a little mala, that had a magnet on it that was stuck to the side of the bench, and it had been there for a very long time. It was covered in cobwebs and two dead spiders, which I brushed off in a not very cool way. They startled me.

But as I looked more closely at the bracelet, I saw there was a charm on it, a half of a heart that read "You." And it had a key that clearly went to the other half of the heart that wasn't there, that must've had a lock, that read "Me." And I could hear within, "Silence in you is the key to Me." If I had ever doubted whether I was supposed to be at that retreat that weekend or not, in that moment, finding that little cheap bracelet with that priceless meaning, I knew I was where I was supposed to be. I knew that it was left for me. To share with you.

What I could feel strongly during that retreat was that it's not just the Silence that we can hear while thinking, but it's the Silence of no thinking. Even just for a second, not following that thought out of this Wholeness, out of this Garden, out of this Eden. Not being tempted to think, just for a moment. To do the opposite of what we usually do—to pause and relax. To stand still. And whether you need to hear "Ram, Ram, Ram" inside to still those thoughts, or "Peace, be still," to hear the stillness after, still, to still those thoughts. Or "Lead us not into temptation" to still those thoughts. Or "Hare Krishna, Hare Ram" to still those thoughts. Or "Hail Mary full of grace." Or "Jesus, I trust in you." Any of those words will take you to the Word. They will take you to the Sound. God's Call to return to His Peace.

In the Presence of Love, the Mind Rests.
In the presence of God, your mind is silent.
In the presence of God, your mind IS Silence.
God heard your prayers before you were born.
Your True prayer, the one behind the words—
to be happy,
to give love,
to be loved,
to be Love.
He's not asking you to do anything but trust.

Give this Silence, this Stillness, your attention,
and It will give you everything.

As Huzur Maharaj Sawan Singh said, "The escape is through the Sound Current." When you hear the Sound of Silence, there are no thoughts. Just like when you pause and hear your mantra. Or when you pause and listen for your breath. What happened to your mind? What happened to you? As that last thought dissolves, so do you, and all that's left is Him. That's all You are. Surrendering to Love's will can be as simple as surrendering to your breath. Surrendering to hearing, to hearing Silence.

> **"As the depth of love increases, the intensity of fear slowly decreases."**
>
> ———
>
> **AMMA**

Focus on this growing Silence. It's not growing; it's boundless. You just seem to be growing more and more aware of It, which means you're going to seem to be growing more and more aware of your purpose, of your passion, of your destiny. The thing you want that seems so impossible, so far off, maybe that's what's destined for you. Maybe that's what's unfolding. Listen. It makes the same sound a rose makes unfolding, blooming. You begin to bloom the moment you come to Silence.

The Sound of Silence is the sound of Abundance.
So keep your inner ear on the Sound,
your inner eye on the Field,
your felt-"I" in Love,
and behold the Harvest.

"Don't you have a saying, 'It's still four months until harvest'?
I tell you, open your eyes and look at the fields! They are ripe
for harvest."

———————

JESUS (JOHN 4:35, NIV)

"There is a statement about hearing and chanting the
maha-mantra [Hare Krishna]: 'It is said that saints have been
able to hear the vibrating strings of the vina in the hands of
Narada, who is always singing the glories of Lord Krsna. Now this
same sound vibration has entered my ears, and I am always feeling
the presence of the Supreme Personality. Gradually I am
becoming bereft of all attachment for material enjoyment.'"

———————

A. C. BHAKTIVEDANTA SWAMI PRABHUPADA,
THE NECTAR OF DEVOTION

The Gravity of God's Love

You don't have to force your way into this Silence.

You don't have to force your way into this Love.

You don't have to force a manifestation.

R E L A X,

into the Force.

That tension you were feeling was the false force;

this Stillness that you've softened into,

this Love,

is THE Force.

It's God.

And God isn't a He, She, or It.

God is an experience—

not something you have to force,

just something you have to feel,

and not stop feeling,

no matter what else you feel,

forever.

THE QUOTES

"For our present troubles are small and won't last very long.
Yet they produce for us a glory that vastly outweighs them and will
last forever!"

———————

2 CORINTHIANS 4:17, NLT

"Your struggles are not because you didn't pray the right way, or
because you didn't pray enough, or because you have weak faith or
insufficient intercessors. It is because God is using you in ways that
you may not understand now, but one day you will. One day you will
see how God used your affliction to prepare you for an
incomparable weight of glory."

———————

DERRIKA DANIELLE (@THEREALSWEETSPOT ON INSTAGRAM)

"A million speak of love, yet how few know, true love is not to lose
remembrance even for an instant."

———————

KABIR

THE PRACTICE

Hear sounds without labeling them. Hear sounds from Silence, not
thoughts. Notice what's (t)here before thoughts. Be That.

Like those burglar alarms that make no noise,
that aren't audible to the trespasser, but sound somewhere else . . .
when I feel invaded by thought,
I close my eyes and I Hear.
I hear this Silence sounding,
and in that Emptiness,

in that Quiet Space,

help gets deployed,

problems get solved,

the right people show up.

This Silence is the helper.

It is the Comforter.

It is Love.

If you could just stop leaving this Love,

if you could just stop forgetting to hear this Love,

you'd start seeing changes.

You'd start seeing yourself as Love,

knowing only Love Is here,

only this Weight

that has no form,

that has no shape,

that has no weight, is here.

But here where you are, It's experienced as a Joyful Gravity,

pulling what's for you,

Destiny,

into Your orbit.

Become aware of the weight of that body,

and relax into It.

Relax into the Love that's (t)here.

The weight is the Love.

When you first become aware of Love where that body is,

the body feels heavier.

It's only because you're more aware of the body.

But close that body's eyes,

and stop giving that weight a shape.

Stop giving it form.

Stop labeling it "weight,"

and just experience it.

Just be the experience.
Surrender fully, and keep surrendering, and keep letting go.
Allow Love to infiltrate,
and be the dream.
The very essence of the world you appear to live in,
It is already.
But you're slowly becoming conscious of It.
It's like this Love is saying, "Are you ready to try my way again?
You're scared because I've brought you through hell.
Your forty days in the desert.
I had to show you that none of your mind tricks,
none of your manipulations, would solve this.
Only Me.
Give Me the rest of the day,
and I'll give you miracles.
No affirmations,
no visualizations,
no imagining.
Just Me, pure, and simple, and full."

In one of his viral videos, That Christian Vlogger, Justin Khoe, said, "I used to think that in order to abide in Christ, I had to read my Bible every day, pray every day, and share my faith every single day. My abiding was depending on me doing something, but this is just wrong. Abiding in Christ is not another work that needs to be performed, but it's a reality to live in. In the same way that one lives in a house and only needs not leave in order to remain in the house."

You are in Christ. And abiding in Him, In It, is simply the decision to not walk away, to not forget to hear.

Listening feels like effort. Hearing is what's always already happening before you can take credit for it, before you can claim doer-ship of it. If you were to hear a car go by outside, you didn't have to try to hear it. It was heard. And then the mind interprets. The mind labels that sound "car" and may comment, "Oh, that's noisy. It's breaking my concentration. I wish I didn't live by a highway."

That's what we're used to hearing inside, that voice. Helpful sometimes, usually not. Can you hear a car go by without labeling it "car" and just be with the hearing? Silently, without narration, without a soundtrack overlay of what you think is happening, or what should be happening, or what shouldn't be happening. Can you just let it happen?

The more you just let each moment, each sound, happen, you start to become aware of the Sound. The Silence, which you never leave. You only imagine you do. You only think you do. When thoughts start, you believe you've left (t)His House, but you have not. Then you just hear again; you hear that you're Home.

Have you ever watched a movie with someone who keeps trying to guess the plot—asking who the characters are, if they're good or bad, or what will happen, as if you've already seen the movie? The mind is like that, questioning the storyline constantly—"I wonder if I should eat first or send that email?"—and when the future-moment arrives where you're aware of that body sending the email, the mind is already asking about and predicting the next future-now. Once you see it, once you give it that look that you'd give your slightly annoying friend, it'll stop, and even if it doesn't right away, it's been seen through. It's guessing game days are over.

And then you stay aware that you're Home, while thoughts are entertained and people are entertained. And situations and problems are entertained; the Silence is the host. The Silence is the house. The Silence is the door. It's the walls. It's the ceiling.

You've never had an experience where the Silence was not primary. The Silence was there first, and then everything else. And you're not having to make It that way, you're not having to force It to be that way. You're waking up to the fact that It is that way. Experiencing Silence more than you're experiencing me, allowing Silence to be louder than your problem, louder than that person you're not looking forward to having to deal with again next week. Louder than everything.

"Between two thoughts, there is a Buddha."

OFTEN ATTRIBUTED TO MILAREPA

And somehow, the simple awareness of It keeps you out of trouble. It keeps you safe. It keeps you protected. It keeps you covered. Even when you're experiencing a trial or a tribulation, while It's happening, you're already hearing the solution, as the Silence, trusting in the Silence appearing as the worldly solution, as the worldly answer. But you heard It first.

When I feel invaded by thought, or by a seeming problem, I close my eyes and I hear. I hear the Silence; the Silence is sounding. And in that emptiness and that quiet space, help gets deployed. Problems get solved. The right people show up. The Silence is the Helper. It's the Comforter. It is Love. It's how God sounds.

"It is written on the gate of heaven: *Nothing in existence is more powerful than destiny. And destiny brought you here, to this page, which is part of your ticket—as all things are— to return to God."*

HAFIZ

1. Practice feeling the energy of your destiny in happiness.
It feels like Love.

2. Practice feeling the energy of your destiny in sadness.
It feels like Love.

3. Practice feeling the energy of your destiny in every step,
in every breath, in every moment. It feels like Love.

4. Look around at what Destiny built. It feels like Love.

*Thoughts change, emotions change; You don't. Ceaseless-Love is
your destiny. It IS Destiny. Feeling It is the path; being It is the
destination.*
. . . And God is just sitting in the corner smiling.
Every time you come back,
every time you come to,
just imagine Him,
legs crossed, looking up from His paper, smiling,
like, "There You are . . . are You ready?
I've been waiting; are you done? Worrying? Fretting?
Good.
Now we can begin at the end.
Just keep coming back to this Love."
That's it.
You're thinking,
you're thinking,
Grace—
You're back in Love.
You're busy, busy, busy . . .
slow down.
LOVE—
hey, slow down.

Calm down.
You've already arrived.
Act like It.
You're already Love(d).
Act like It.

PART THREE

Being Love

"At a distance you only see My Light, come closer
and know that I am You."

ATTRIBUTED TO RUMI

"One cannot look at the mystery.
One can only look from the mystery
Because one is the mystery."

WU HSIN

Can you Love like This for the rest of the day?
That's a trick question.
There is no "day."
There's only Now,
beyond the word "now."
Beyond time,
beyond space,
just Love, that You're being,
And you don't need to extend It or remember It.
Just This is enough.
You are enough.
Love Surrounds You.
It is You.

"I merged so completely with Love, and was so fused, that I became Love, and Love became me."

ATTRIBUTED TO RUMI

"The melting of everything in Spirit is a state no one can describe. A great bliss is felt—external fullness of joy and knowledge and love. The love of God, the love of the Spirit, is an all-consuming love. Once you have experienced it, it shall lead you on and on in the eternal realms."

PARAMHANSA YOGANANDA, *MAN'S ETERNAL QUEST*

"'Father, there is little to tell.' She spread her graceful hands in a deprecatory gesture. 'My consciousness has never associated itself with this temporary body. Before I came on this earth, Father, "I was the same." As a little girl, "I was the same." I grew into womanhood; still "I was the same." When the family in which I had been born made arrangements to have this body married, "I was the same." And, Father, in front of you now, "I am the same." Ever afterward, though the dance of creation change around me in the hall of eternity, "I shall be the same."'"

PARAMHANSA YOGANANDA DESCRIBING
ANANDAMAYI MA IN *AUTOBIOGRAPHY OF A YOGI*

This Feels Like the Way
Because It Is (Real Self-Love)

It's all Prayer,
when you stay aware of God's Presence, when you're constantly calling
His Name inside.
Not because He's not there, and you're wanting
Him to come to you,
but because He is there and you're wanting your attention to stay there,
to stay Here, on Him.
On Love.
On Silence.
On God. This works.
TRUST.

THE QUOTE

"We pinch ourselves to know that we are alive in this life.
Considerable joy, considerable joy. All of us one, one consciousness.
That is the way in which the world could right itself. You start with
your peace, your love, your compassion, and go from there and
then love everything. Love everything. Even those thoughts."

—————————

RAM DASS

THE PRACTICE

Close that body's eyes and know, "This isn't me; this is Me." This sense of presence isn't personal; It's Universal.

I Am that "I Am."
I Am that Love.
With that body's eyes open, continue to feelingly-know.
Each day this week,
sit that body down.
Sit it up straight,
close its eyes, and know that that's Shiva sitting there.
That's Hanuman.
That's Krishna,
Rama,
Jesus,
Buddha, sitting there.
That's how sitting becomes easier—
when you tap into your highest level of consciousness,
the One that's been sitting for lifetimes,
that's been mediating for millions of years.
Tap into that place inside,
the One that knows what to do,
that doesn't need to read,
that doesn't need questions answered,
because there are no questions in this Silence, no words, no world.
Just Love.

I constantly receive messages from listeners and readers about the inability to love themselves. It's hard to love something that is ever-changing, fluctuating, nonexistent, truly. You can't Love what's not there. You can Love only what's here, seemingly looking out through that body's eyes right now. That's not you. That's God. That's Love. That's Buddha seeing these words, hearing the sounds from the Silence. The hearing itself is the Silence. That's Jesus sitting (t)here, eyes opened, meditating, hearing these, His own, Your own, words repeated inside. That's Guru Nanak. That's Sri Ramana Maharshi, Ram Dass, Saint Francis of Assisi. Love their presence where you are. That's real Self-Love. Feel their presence where you are. Feel your presence as theirs because there is no difference. The same Love you're practicing, they all practiced it. They all walked this path. They're walking it with you as you, looking through your eyes, experiencing as you, all of your ancestors. Even the one who most recently passed, they're with you, in you. You are all this one Love, this one Consciousness appearing as the many, and you're beginning to remember that.

Moment by moment,
these conscious moments turn into conscious days,
turn into conscious weeks,
months,
years.
A conscious life,
a lucid life,
a blessed one.
But because of our lucidity,
we see more,
we feel more.
The good and the bad because we're being The More.
We are That, and we trust That.

In that trust, we find our security, we find purpose, we find ourselves serving and giving more than receiving. Praying ceaselessly, swaying. Constantly lost in this Love.

This week, make sure you take some time—not for reading, necessarily, not for watching something, even spiritual, or listening to me or anything else. Your true teacher is the Silence, and you have to sit with It. There's no other way. No matter how boring It seems to be or how scary It seems, no matter how much that body wants to get up and do anything else, sit it down, sit it up straight, close its eyes, and know that that's God sitting there.

Like Sri Sri Ravi Shankar said, "All your ambitions and achievements are connected with others, with the world either to show off, prove yourself, or to provide." Just for a moment, imagine there is no one to appreciate your achievements nor to support your ambition, and you will find yourself to be calm and free. You'll find yourself listening. That's all meditation is. That's what Adyashanti, a contemporary spiritual teacher, called it during a talk, "a profound willingness to listen." He said, "Don't try to be silent. Instead, just listen." He said, "But listening is a humble thing because the mind wants to come in there and it wants to hear its own voice, but you're listening for God's voice now." That's the only voice that matters, and It's getting louder and louder. The Sound of Silence is becoming clearer and clearer. You're becoming happier and happier for no reason, smiling more for no reason. This feels like the way because It is.

> "Other than what you're thinking and believing, you're okay. Right?"
>
> ———
>
> **BYRON KATIE**

There's a Silence there that's not thinking and believing. There's an Awareness (t)here. Take sacred moments this week to close those eyes and notice this Awareness. It doesn't matter if thoughts are present; the Awareness is still here. It's still on. It's aware of the presence of thoughts.

It's aware of the absence of thoughts. It's aware of these words, it's aware of your breathing now, and we bow to this Awareness. We pray,

"Eternal Awareness, You are the only Presence. Your sacred name is 'I Am.' Your Perfection is just a realization away, not even a breath away. As consciousness unfolds, give now your Grace and forgive unawareness. Let the mind be an avenue of awareness. Free of thinking, free of belief. For you are the only Presence, the only Power, and Eternal, Timeless Perfection. And so it is."

GIL MICHAELS

No negative thinking.
No one can stop what this awareness is doing in your life.
What has been set into motion by your constant turning,
and trusting and loving, starting with yourself.
Thank God. Thank You.

One Who Is Everywhere Is Joyous; One Who Is Nowhere Is Free

"You must come to conclusion, I am unborn,
I was unborn and I remain unborn."

NISARGADATTA MAHARAJ

THE QUOTES

"The minute you identify yourself as something, you are not nothing and you are not everything; you have limited yourself."

SWAMI SATCHIDANANDA

"When we know who we are, we're everybody and we're free."

KRISHNA DAS

THE PRACTICE

Rock and sway between these two mantras: "I am nowhere, I am everywhere" and "I am nothing, I am everything." The moment you make the felt-connection with Love, you are beyond the body. You are no longer attached to it. You're free, and that freedom feels like Joy. You are everywhere and nowhere. You are everyone and no one. You are the invisible, formless, boundless Love appearing as the countless visible forms. And because you know This, because you ARE This, that body smiles. Love is felt as its very being.

On my way back from a Ram Dass retreat on Maui in 2021, I was swiping through my notes from years past. I like to feel back into where I was at different seeming times, what I was practicing, and what I knew to be true. And I came across a mantra that I used for a while—"Nowhere."

That was it. That was the whole mantra. *Nowhere*. A longer form of it would be *I am nowhere*.

*And then dropping the words and just recognizing that I am
not in the scene.
There is a scene, there is an appearance, but I am not in it.
I am nowhere. It's a beautiful way to detach and feel into what
is beyond the appearance.
It would've been equally powerful and true to use the mantra
"I am everywhere."
It's the same thing.* **Whether you're everywhere or nowhere,
you're not somewhere or someone.**
*In a moment, close your eyes and feel into nowhere.
There's a sense of that body there,
a sense of location,
but it's just a sense.
Say in your mind, feel
"I am nowhere," or simply "Nowhere."*

Allow that sense of a body to just be one other object in your vast, boundless, nowhere in particular but everywhere, awareness.

Open that body's eyes and look around while thinking, "Nowhere"—you are present, but not as that body. As the Hindu saint Nisargadatta Maharaj would say, "You are simply conscious of not having a body."

Osho said, "Toss attachment for body aside, realizing I am everywhere. One who is everywhere is joyous." When someone asked him how to detach from the body, he said, "If your house is on fire, you will not ask anyone, you will not go seeking a master to ask how to come out of it. If the house is on fire, you will simply get out of it. You will not lose a single moment. You will not search for the teacher; you will not consult the scriptures. And you will not try to choose in what ways one has to come out, what means have to be adopted, and which door is the right door. These things are irrelevant when the house is on fire. When you know what attachment is, the house is on fire. You can put it aside. And there is no need to ask how. It is absolutely a fire, a hell. You can jump out of it. And the moment you toss aside the attachment, you will realize you are everywhere. Because of this attachment you feel you are limited by the body. It is not the body which is limiting you; it is your attachment to it. It is not the body which is making a barrier between you and the reality; it is your attachment to it. Once you know [that] the attachment is not there, there is no body to you. Rather, the whole existence becomes your body; your body becomes a part of the total existence. Then it is not separate."

Where there is no sense of separation, there is only felt-Love, a GoOD feeling.

This God feeling you allow yourself to become aware of, behind closed eyes at first, and then with eyes open.

And the rocking, smiling, hand over your heart, gentle bowing, inner alertness, and inner hearing are all ways to detach from the sense of separateness, from the sense of body identification.

These are like the snapping fingers that break the hypnosis, the alarm clock that wakes you out of the dream. The mantra "Nowhere" is simply just another alarm clock to remind you of what you're not, of where you're not, of who you're not. And then sometimes, you'll feel yourself as everywhere.

> "Love says, 'I am everything.' Wisdom says, 'I am nothing.'
> Between the two, my life flows."
>
> ———————
>
> **NISARGADATTA MAHARAJ**

Rock and sway between these two mantras this week.
"I am nowhere. I am everywhere" and "I am nothing. I am everything."
All as true as words can be.
Silence is the whole truth.

Bonus: Who is the one rocking?
What is swaying?
Who is repeating the mantras?
Who is aware?

Be(yond) Here Now

You've been feeling like the weight of the world is on your
shoulders,
and yet you have no shoulders.
And there is no world.
Be(come) Light.
Just for this moment,
leave that body where it is,
and be beyond "here" with me.
This is no longer "be here now."
This is "Be BEYOND here, now."
Because even "here" is a concept.
Even "here" we are imagining.
Here is not here.
And you know what takes you beyond here?
Hearing.
What can you hear beyond here,
beyond that room,
that space you appear to be in?
Listen for what's beyond it.
As if everything you see is a veil,
including "you."

Come out
of that mind,
of that form,
in Jesus's Name.

THE QUOTE

"Be here now."

———————

RAM DASS

THE PRACTICE

Affirm: "I am the power that is in the body" (Shri Ranjit Maharaj, in Andrew Vernon, *You Are He*).

You don't have to call to you what's already here.
God is already here, saying, "I am the power that is in the body."
Keep saying it until you start feeling it,
until you become aware of the pure feeling that says "I am the
power that is in the body,"
without the words "I am the power that is in the body." You just
start being that power, recognizing that you are that power.
Herb Fitch says:

> *"Do you see that we as human beings in the flesh are still in*
> *the womb of creation?*
>
> *"This is the womb; we haven't been born yet. When we come*
> *out of me, when me dies, and I is born, we are reborn of the*
> *Spirit. We begin our New Horizon. We see His universe instead*
> *of the world of our limited human minds. We see His universe*
> *where only harmony exists. We see with a Christ Mind, the*
> *reborn mind and we see what Is, instead of what we have*

imagined to be. We walk through the visions of this false mind and we see: His love, His peace, His truth, His universe, His creation, His being. We see God face to face. There is no God and me. There is no God and you. There never has been."

There never was.
That quiet Feeling there that announces,
"I am alive, I am here," but silently,
that's God.
Everyone you think you know feels This,
Is This,
but it's your responsibility to be This.
Mother Teresa is known to have said, "How sad it is when someone comes to you looking for Jesus and all they see is you."
You can take my mantra "Only Love is here" and switch it up—
Another name for Love is Jesus—"Only Jesus Is."
Only the Christ Is.
And feel His being,
His heart,
His mind,
where yours appears to be.
Know that only That is where your neighbor appears to be.
That's how you Love them as yourself, because That's all they are.
Just as if you were dreaming at night and met your neighbor in your dream—upon awakening you'd realize: "The neighbor was myself. Just my mind playing as two." Your spouse, that's you, too.
Love pretending to be two. If you know there's only one there, there will be no conflict. Just Love in form.
Whenever I am overthinking something,
worried about something,
there's a pause
and then an awareness of

"I am this Presence,"

purely, with no thought,

just naked "I am"-ness.

Not even "I am breathing."

Because the breathing is happening seemingly out here,

and I am back here.

I'm just . . .

I just am.

There's not even a "here."

Even "here" is imagined.

And then there is a knowing,

not a believing,

but a knowing

that this "I am"

is God.

And then whatever was concerning me, concerning Nikki,

is seen as like a bogeyman.

It's not true.

It's not real.

It can't harm Me.

It can't touch Me.

Only this Power is, and I am That.

Not "I have to appeal to That."

Not "I have to pray to That."

Not "I have to beg for That."

Not even "I have to surrender to That."

I already am That.

You already are That.

Whatever I am,

you are,

because there's only this One here,

and so you feel this presence,

and the moment you're feeling it,
you're not that body anymore.
You are not in the scene anymore.
You have no shape, no form, no color.
You have no age, no weight.
No problem.
That problem was solved before you even became aware of it.
Do you hear me?
A thought will say "How?" or "There's no way!" or "You don't even
know what problem I have."
But I do because I have it, too.
I am you, too.
The problem isn't (t)here.
Nothing is.
Relax that stomach and feel those shoulders come down.
That was the only problem you had.
That tension, that tightness, that imagined weight,
That imagined wait you've placed yourself in.
You're not in that, either.
You're not in a season of waiting or in a season of hiding.
Come out.
And take It all the way this time.

Don't Sing the Sadness Anymore

The tears you cry are not because you're lost;

they're because you're found.

You are found in Love.

Love sees you,

and you cry when you look away.

You cry when your mind tells you that Love is not (t)Here.

You cry when you see and hear things that aren't truly (t)Here.

But when you're fully Here,

like you are right now,

you find Love,

again.

And you hear It.

THE QUOTES

"Everything is clapping today. Light, sound, motion, all movement."

_____

HAFIZ

"Don't sing the sadness anymore. Call out that you have been given both the answer and an understanding of the question."

RUMI

THE PRACTICE

"Hear the sound of one hand clapping."

ZEN KOAN

You can't hear it,
but the whole world is clapping for you.
Take a bow,
Smile,
and feel through what you see,
to the Celebration that's (t)here.
Let your ear lead you to this Love.
Listen until you feel the Comforter that Jesus promised you.
Every time you want something,
*feel It saying—***"That is Me. You don't want that; you want Me."**

Every time you look at anything, hear—*"Remember, that's not really there, I Am. Remember, they're not really there, I Am."*

You are clapping for yourself for BEing your Self.

"The Divine Mother revealed to me in the Kāli temple that it was She who had become everything. She showed me that everything was full of Consciousness. The Image was Consciousness, the altar was Consciousness, the water-vessels were Consciousness, the door-sill was Consciousness, the marble floor was Consciousness—all was Consciousness.

"I found everything inside the room soaked, as it were, in Bliss—the Bliss of Satchidananda. I saw a wicked man in front of the Kāli temple; but in him also I saw the Power of the Divine Mother vibrating. That was why I fed a cat with the food that was to be offered to the Divine Mother. I clearly perceived that the Divine Mother Herself had become everything—even the cat. The manager of the temple garden wrote to Mathur Babu saying that I was feeding the cat with the offering intended for the Divine Mother. But Mathur Babu had insight into the state of my mind. He wrote back to the manager: 'Let him do whatever he likes. You must not say anything to him.'"

SRI RAMAKRISHNA

I've been going to the sauna three times a week, and it is amazing. Because I'm a chronic multitasker, I also use that time either to meditate on the Silence or to chant—which holds my attention not only on the Silence but also on this Love, this Bliss, this Joy, beyond the heat and the sweating and the thoughts of "Is it time for me to leave this terrible room yet?" And it's so beautiful how Bliss is still perceived beyond the discomfort and impatience. How the Silence is still perceived, how the Love never goes, even when the body is in a state of "No, thank you." I'm still like, "Yes! Hare Rama, Hare Ram, Ram, Ram, Hare, Hare, Hare Krishna, Hare Krishna, Krishna, Krishna, Hare, Hare." It's like being at a Kirtan (congregational devotional singing) with a group of people joyfully singing and clapping, but there's nothing here. The sauna booth is as empty as Jesus's tomb. No body here. Only Love. That's what He was teaching us.

What's the sound of one hand clapping?
That's the sound of success.
If you want more of It,
you have to hear more of This.
You have to hear the Silence beyond the world clapping,
beyond the desire you hold of hearing the world clapping for you.
You have to hear God clapping.
He already is.
Love's always been clapping.
You keep bowing.

Feel Love saying—"That thorn in your side (that job, that illness,
that person)
is to bring you closer to Me,
to lock you inside of Me,
inside of My Love,
inside of My Healing,
inside of My Will,
so that you'll stop leaving.
Don't let the appearance of this world make you forget that
you're in Me.
That I'm all around you.
Just listen,
when the noise becomes too much,
listen for Me.

When you listen to sound,

the very listening is Me.

The Silence and Sound are not separate.

The Formless and Form are not separate.

I Am not separate from you.

Surrender.

Soften.

Relax into Me—

the fulfillment of your greatest Desire."

What Is Yours Will Know
Your Face (Original Face)

"To hear the Original Plan, (Y)our Original Plan before
you took birth, you have to become Silence."

———————

LOVE

Things have already "come together,"
"unfolded,"
"fallen into place,"
but they will appear to take time in your experience.
It's all here, always now,
the storm and the rainbow,
but the purpose of your experience is to live moment to seeming
moment,
in and AS this Love.
That's what you're missing.

As often as you notice you forget to consult with Me,
to listen for Me before acting,
you forget to be this Love.
If you could just Love more,
you would see more of what's already Here.
You would stop trying to paint your own doors on walls
and, finally, look and see My doors standing wide open for you.
Pass through.

THE QUOTES

"What is mine shall know my face."

———————

JOHN BURROUGHS

"If I can't stop thinking, maybe I can just let my thoughts go by
without getting all caught up in them. Feel the breeze on your face
or your neck? See how it's going by? You're not all hung up with it.
You don't have to see where each breeze goes. You don't have to
look quickly to see if it hit those trees over there. It's breezes, and
they're just going by. Make your thoughts like those breezes, those
little breezes . . . just going by."

———————

RAM DASS

"Who am I?
I am myself a word spoken by God.
Can God speak a word that does not have any meaning?"

———————

THOMAS MERTON

THE PRACTICE

Whenever you notice doubt, notice Me, too—your Self.

> "What did your face look like before your parents were born?"
>
> ZEN KOAN

The way you have no doubt that you're alive?
You have to have THAT kind of faith that Love is providing for you.
Can you have no doubt about that?
No doubt that you're being guided?
No doubt you're being sheltered, protected?
When you get quiet,
when you "be still and know" that you're aware, that you're alive,
you're simultaneously acknowledging the presence of God.
The aliveness and the presence of God are One.
The "I Am" and the presence of God are One.
Your presence is His.
In that moment, just as you don't doubt that you're alive,
you also don't doubt that you're being carried.
By your Self, back to your Self.

Divine Love is lightly here. Can you feel It? It may be experienced as an ever-deepening sigh of relief or like a vibration in your feet, hands, or heart. Your mind will say, "No, this can't be it." It's not very exciting; it's quite subtle. You'd miss it if you didn't know what you were looking and listening for.

Remember, I listen for the feeling of Love. I listen for the Silence that's doing the "hearing." And when I find It, I find Love. I shared this with a friar on a silent retreat during one of our daily check-ins, and he said, "That's Grace, to be able to feel God like you're feeling Him right now."

You're already free.
That's what you're hearing right now.
And when the mind comes back in a moment,
trying to get you to remember what you're supposed to be anxious about or worried about,
it won't take you on a trip for a whole day or a whole week anymore.
Just for a few moments—you'll be fooled, you'll be hypnotized, seemingly,
but then you'll be back, here with Me.
Here with your grandma,
your great-grandma,
that favored aunt.
Whether they appear to be alive or transitioned,
this Love is them.
When you're here,
you're with them.
You're one with them.
When you're here,
you're one with God.
You're home in God.
You can feel Her Hands on you,
and you know that there's never anywhere that you've gone to,
and nowhere that you'll go,
that this Love won't be there already,
comforting you,
strengthening you,
giving you the energy or the courage to carry on to get you through another day.
To help you inspire another smile.
All the paths you've walked,
are walking,

or will walk are here.
All your victories,
the past ones,
the ones you haven't lived yet,
they're Here.
The things you think you want and need are already Here.
You can't see them,
but you can feel them,
or you can hear them as the Silence,
as the ringing in the Silence. Calling you.
I feel them.
I feel what's yours as Love.
And our work is wanting this Love more than anything else,
until even that desire dissolves,
until even the one that had that desire dissolves.
So you can see through it, all of it.
In truth, there's nothing to see through.
Even taking the moment to stop and try to see through it is
an illusion.
This Love is already (t)here before the thought.
Nothing ever happened. Nothing is happening.

"As it was in the beginning, is now, and ever shall be:
world without end. Amen."

GLORY BE PRAYER

"Till the false is seen as false, Truth is not."

JIDDU KRISHNAMURTI

Continue, God

> "In the beginning the ignorant devotee says, 'I am His.'
> When He grows in Bhakti he says, 'I am Thine.' When he
> develops the highest Bhakti, he exclaims in joy and
> rapturous ecstasy and delight, 'I am Thou.'"
>
> **SWAMI SIVANANDA,** *BHAKTI AND SANKIRTAN*

You are what the Christ has transformed Itself into.
It's become you,
me,
your neighbors,
your friends,
and your "enemies."
And this year we're loving ALL of our Self—
remembering that where ourselves appear,
only God is.
Only Joy is,
right behind the person,
right behind their eyes,

beyond those hands.

Look down at them . . .

right beyond those hands

is His hand,

stretched out still. (Isaiah 9:12, 17)

Stilling you

enough to feel His Grace,

as that breath that you just took.

And that one.

And that one.

Continue this way.

This is The Way.

The Way of "not two"—not a "you" and a "Her"

but allowing for that seeming duality because it's sweet,

It makes the Love richer—

All the while knowing that Love begins with two and ends as One.

It makes life GoOD.

THE QUOTES

"There is writing happening

Maybe that's hard for you to understand

I am here but 'I' am not here.

I am writing but 'I' am not writing

Inside of me in the heart cave is a

mantra going on that reminds me

who I really am

Over and over again

in this inner place

I am"

RAM DASS, *BE HERE NOW*

THE PRACTICE

This week, catch yourself talking, and notice, "I'm not talking." Walking, state inwardly, "I'm not walking." Working, "I'm not working." Hear the Silence as the body continues to talk, walk, and work. **You see it, but you're not it.**

That breath you just took,
and that one, is by God's Grace.
It's by His Love that you continue to breathe through that growing smile.
We have to let this Love be like breathing,
constantly here.
Breathe in and breathe out,

but let it be Love coming in, and Love going out.
This whole life is receiving and giving,
receiving and giving.

How often do you see someone's open hand and hold it? Mark Gladman, also known as Monk In Docs, said, "Look at your hands for a moment. There are people out there whose hands yours will fit into. That's why you have hands, to hold the hands of others, to lift up others by their hands, to place things in the hands of others, to work with your hands alongside others. May God give us eyes to see the open hands and the willingness to hold them as long as they need."

Isaiah 58:10-11 says, "And if you spend yourselves on behalf of the hungry and satisfy the needs of the oppressed, then your light will rise in the darkness, and your night will become like the noonday. The Lord will guide you always; He will satisfy your needs in a sun-scorched land and will strengthen your frame. You will be like a well-watered garden, like a spring whose waters never fail."

Continue, God, to do with me what you're doing with me.

Continue to let me serve You.
Continue to let me hear You.

> **"I will not let the small things start killing me again."**
>
> ———
>
> **WILLIAM BORTZ**

You're no longer letting the small things distract you from the big thing, the real thing.

> **"If you feed people, you will never be hungry."**
>
> ———
>
> **ATTRIBUTED TO MAHARAJJI**

Maharajji wasn't just talking about food. He was talking about the Substance beyond food, that Essence behind food, behind smiles, compassion, offering a hand.

You continue to be kind in a seemingly unkind world.
You continue to be Light.
You continue to feel Love,
to be Love in those spaces that up until a moment ago,
you weren't looking forward to going back into.
But now you know you have a purpose,
to be His Love in those places,
to be an open hand in those places,
to see through those places.

Instead of squaring up,
instead of tightening up, relax in those places,
to be like you're being right now with me in those places,
to be who you are when you're by yourself in those places.
Who are you when you're just with You?
When you're being Love?

> "The truth is that you're always alone. Even when you're with others, you're essentially alone."
>
> ———
>
> MOOJI

But it's a beautiful aloneness.
It's not psychological.
You're not alone anymore as a person.
You're alone as everything, as the only One.
All the various others are only forms of the single Self.
That's why Saint Seraphim of Sarov was able to say, "Acquire the Spirit of Peace, and a thousand souls around you will be saved."
It's because you are the souls around you.
And in this spirit, the giving is receiving.
The receiving is giving.
They become one.
When you see someone winning in your life,
you won.
And if you can continue to see things this way,
to breathe this way,
how you are right now,

then you'll continue to have, in the words of Saint Augustine, "a mind through which Christ thinks, a heart through which Christ loves, a voice through which Christ speaks, and a hand through which Christ helps."

You feel different because you are different.
It's hard for you to do the things that other people do,
the routines that other people have,
because you're not other people.
You're not a people.
So stop trying to be a people.
Stop trying to fit in.
Stop trying to keep up.
You live this Christhood,
and you be your own,
you be His own,
and you'll lift everyone with you.
You'll bring everyone with you,
but you're not focusing on them—that's just the side effect.
You just chant and mind your business.
You feel Love where you see yourself,
where you see others,
and you mind your business.
You see your business, and you feel Love,
that's how you mind your business.
And the right actions happen,
but really nothing is happening.
And as long as you remember nothing is happening,
even while you are in action,
you won.

Let "I Love You" Become Your Breath

This is the ancient prayer of the Breath,
of the Heart.
The prayer that He prays in you,
constantly,
for you to hear,
to be calmed,
and to be victorious.

THE QUOTES

"So neither he who plants nor he who waters is anything, but only God who gives the growth. He who plants and he who waters are one, and each will receive his wages according to his labor. For we are God's fellow workers. You are God's field, God's building."

1 CORINTHIANS 3:7-9, ESV

"To say the Word *lā ilāha* and to push the world away, to say the Word *illAllāhu* and to bring it down into your heart, to experience bliss, to say it without saying it, to raise and lower it breath after breath, to say it without saying it, to raise and lower it breath after breath, until the liberation in the Word *illAllāhu* resonates alone."

─────────

BAWA MUHAIYADDEEN

THE PRACTICE

Say, "I Love You" on every breath. If there's something in your life you don't like right now, say, "I Love You, ____," on every breath.

"We have a job to do: plant the seeds and trust God to bring the growth."

─────────

SCOTT MACINTYRE

As 1 Corinthians 3:7 says, "Neither he who plants nor he who waters is anything, but only God who gives the growth."

He who plants and he who waters are one,
and each will receive his wages according to his labor,
for we are God's fellow workers.
You are God's field,
God's building,
God's breathing in and out,
gently,
effortlessly,
you were unaware of it before,
but you're aware of it now.
Now gently and peacefully and mentally, begin repeating,
"I Love You."

On every inhalation, "I Love You."
On every exhalation, allowing the "I Love You" to match the flow,
the natural flow, of your breath,
not trying to match the flow of your breath with the "I Love Yous."
Not manipulating the breath in any way,
just setting the "I Love You" on the breath.
For even more feeling, more Love, add a name of God—
Jesus, I Love You.
Yeshua, I Love You.
Yahweh, Jehovah, Allah, Mother, I Love You.
Rama, Krishna, I Love You. Pick one Name, I Love You.

If there is someone in your life right now who you're finding it hard to Love, like a spouse, a parent, a partner,"___, (the thing or name), I Love You." Feel Love for that which you have forgotten is only Love, too.

Feel that on every inhalation, on every exhalation. Kabir, the great poet-saint from India, said, "The breath that does not repeat the Name of God is a wasted breath."

This morning, I opened Luisa Piccarreta's *Book of Heaven* to a random page. I want to emphasize how many pages are in this book, 1,789 pages, and I opened to this page, which just happens to be dated October 4, 1925, the day and year that my Grandma Maxine was born:

Before flipping to that page, I had closed my eyes and mentally requested a clear message to confirm my practice, the practice I share here with you, the practice of planting seeds, of Love, whether in the form of "Hare Krishna" or in the form of "Not my will but Yours," or simply "I Love You, I Love You, I Love You."

"Repeating the same good serves to form the water with which to water the seed of the virtues. Everything that our Lord has done is suspended in the Divine Will, in waiting, to give itself to creatures.

"I was fusing myself in the Most Holy Will of God according to my usual way, and while going around in It to place my 'I love You' upon all things, I wished that my Jesus would see or hear nothing but my 'I love You,' or through this 'I love You' of mine. And while repeating the singsong of my 'I love You,' I thought to myself: "It shows that I am really a little child, who can say nothing but the little story she has learned. And then, what good comes to me by repeating 'I love You, I love You . . .' over and over again?" But while I was thinking of this, my adorable Jesus came out from within my interior, showing my 'I love You' impressed everywhere in all of His Divine Person: on His lips, on His face, on His forehead, in His eyes, in the middle of His breast, on the back and in the center of the palms of His hands, on the tips of His fingers—in sum, everywhere. And with a tender tone, He told me: 'My daughter, aren't you happy that none of the 'I love You's' that come out of you go lost, but all remain impressed in me? And then, do you know what good comes to you by repeating them? You Must Know that when the soul decides to do some good, to exercise a virtue, she forms the seed of that virtue. By repeating those acts, she forms the water with which to water that seed in the earth of her heart; and the more often she repeats them, the more she waters that seed, and the plant grows beautiful and green, in such a way that it quickly produces the fruits of that seed.'"

———————

LUISA PICCARRETA, *THE BOOK OF HEAVEN*

Try to sustain this powerful breath prayer this week as you go
about your work,
As you drive,
as you eat,
as you email,
as you listen.
Raise it and lower it,
breath after breath.
Say it without saying it,
feel it on every breath.
Anandamayi Ma did this for many years on her way to perfection,
On her way to effortlessness in this.
"Hari" was on every breath,
every inhale,
every exhale,
no matter what was happening,
even if she was chanting something different outwardly.
She said that even if she was singing a different Name of God,
a different song of praise,
"Hari" was on the breath.
"Hari" became her breath.
Let "I love you" become your breath.

Turn On the Lights

Relax your shoulders, breathe in Love, and as you breathe out Love, feel your entire body light up. Feel your being turn on. You're aware of everything around you, ambient sounds, the sensations in the body, my words. You're aware of the Silence in the room you're in, the Silence around my words repeating within you, the thoughts there, the Silence they come from.

You're aware of this tingly Aliveness in your feet. You're aware of the Stillness in your thighs. You're aware of the Love within and without. Look out at the forms around you, of which the body is one, while feeling Love. This is the practice. It would be as if you had a toothache right now: no matter what you were doing, no matter what you were looking at, no matter who you were talking to, your mind would be on that toothache.

Note: Love is never "off"; your attention just isn't "on" It!

Looking,
wanting,
praying,
waiting . . .
This is all we do,
until we are called to Be.

The Silence has called you into Itself,
beyond your problems,
beyond your needs,
beyond your prayers.
And It's holding you (t)here, softly,
as you become more like It, Holy.
As you begin to appreciate It, fully.
As you begin to Love It as It Loves you,
to call on It, as It called you.
LIGHTS ON.
You were calling your Self.
Only You are here.

THE QUOTES

"May all that has been reduced to noise in you become music again."

_____

UNKNOWN

"There is only one step, no other steps."

_____

JIDDU KRISHNAMURTI

THE PRACTICE

Begin to pray the prayer you pray most often, the mantra you chant. And now, turn on the Love.

Become aware of Love while those words are present,
and notice the difference.
Notice the Awareness.
Notice the connection.

It's like you turned on the Light.
The Light was off.
That's how we usually pray.
It's how we usually chant.
Then you turned It on,
and all that was inharmonious in you
became harmonious again.

You could hear again not just the words of your prayer, of your mantra, but the Love.

Instead of praying while thinking that this prayer won't be answered. Or "How can this prayer be answered?" Or "What am I going to eat later?" Or "I need to get dressed. I don't have time to do this. Let me hurry and finish." You pray while listening to the words of the prayer. While feeling the Love. You pray as if God is right (t)here listening, because You are.

> "To listen is to lean in, softly, with a willingness to be changed by what we hear."
>
> **MARK NEPO**

The Love is more important than any words the mind can put together, than any words the mind can parrot. We use the words to hold us here, where God is. We're not chanting or praying to please God, or to sway God to do something, because He's already doing everything. We pray to attune ourselves to this Energy, to align ourselves.

> "All powers are hidden within the Self and they manifest when you connect to your consciousness."
>
> **SRI SRI RAVI SHANKAR**

When you connect to your Consciousness, you see that even the concept of God is Māyā, illusion. Everything you can think of, you can conceive of, is Māyā. So you let go of everything, of every thought, of every desire, of every prayer. Drop into this place beyond prayer, into this pure Awareness, this felt-Knowing. It has no problems. So there are no prayers to pray, there is no one to pray them, and there is no one to pray them to. Just this Love aware of Itself.

Aware of breathing,
of thinking, again.
Aware of wanting,
of praying,
aware of waiting.

> "God is not just found in your blessings, answered prayers, and miracles. God is also in the waiting. He's in your moments of silence. He's in the seeking, asking, and surrendering. He's in the hard times. Even if you don't see or feel it, the Lord is with you and He will never forsake you. He will never change."
>
> **JONALYN SAN DIEGO**

When this Love is aware of being human, like It is where you appear to be right now, all of this comes into play. Prayer is in play. Mantra is in play. Practice is in play. Thirst and hunger are in play.

The Catholic priest and author Father Thomas Dubay said, "Our deepest hungers are not for food and drink, not for amusements and recreations, not for property and wardrobes, not for notoriety and gossip. We hunger for truth, we thirst to drink beauty, we yearn to celebrate, we seek to delight, we stretch out to love and to be loved. This is why anything less than everything is not enough." This is why you're hurting. This is why you're tired. This is why you feel lonely. This is why you feel short-tempered. This is why you know there's more.

You're hearing The Call. Most don't hear This Call. They don't feel this Light because they're too busy in the world. You're busy in the world, too, but you're also busy about the Father's business, and you judge yourself because of how often you forget. But this week, let's praise ourselves for how often we remember. Let's thank God for the Grace that we're even able to practice, that you're able to be aware of Love sometimes. The moment you're aware of It, you're aware of It always.

There's only one moment. There's only one breath. Just this one step that you keep taking. Rock with me backward and forward, like we're at that wall in Jerusalem, that we're praying a silent prayer. We're praying the prayer of Silence. We're praying the prayer of Love. Every time we lean forward, we lean into Love. Everywhere our eyes fall, we know that's God appearing. That's God appearing. That's God. He's God, and she's God, and I'm God, and this is all God, which means it's all good. No matter how it looks, no matter how this body feels, no matter what the senses report, only God is here. Only God is here. Only God is here. God is saying, "It's the Love that counts. It's the Love that matters. It's the Love I hear. It's the Love that prays, that breathes." Right now, breathe like you know who you are, like you know whose you are. Smile like you know where you're going. You don't . . . you're walking by faith, not by sight, but you're making it. He's made a Way. Just breathe, in every step. Just breathe, in every seeming moment today, in every email you open, in every anxious thought, just breathe.

HE KNOWS. What is your prayer? Close your eyes and pray it. And now this time, I want you to say it again, but not to yourself. But to Him. He's right here, closer than that breath you just took. You feel that shift? From dead words to the living Word. You have to pray with Love. With the awareness of this Presence. While on a silent retreat in Tampa, Florida (see Week 30), during one of our verbal check-ins, I asked my spiritual director, Father Kevin (a friar of fifty-plus years), how he experiences the presence of God. Silently, he picked up his Bible and he held it up to his chest, right over his heart, and he started rocking back and forth. And all I could do was smile—he was speaking my language! And then I went into the Silence, no questions left, only Love.

Until Now You Have Asked for Nothing in My Name

Every time you're noticing thoughts, pause and come back Here. When you dissolve the thoughts, you're dissolving the problem. Whatever it was you were thinking about is also clearing. The sky of your mind is clearing, revealing the twinkling star, the Son that you are.

Until now you were sleepwalking.
Sleep praying.
But it's a new dawn.
Welcome to the GoOD life,
to your life in God,
in His Name,
in the Sun.
You're remembering—

1. that you don't need anything you Have
2. that hearing the Name, (t)His Silence, or this Divine Tone in the Silence, IS praying
3. that hearing It while "asking" is Alchemy
4. that you don't even have to "ask," because at all times you're hearing what He's giving

5. that there's no hearing outside of This
6. that there's no living outside of This
7. that Love's always on.

THE QUOTES

"First, He prepares the ground, and then He plants the Seed of the True Name."

_____

SRI GURU GRANTH SAHIB (SIKH BIBLE)

"What he [Jesus] says is *pray beshemi*, pray within my shem, within my sound, within my atmosphere. You could say within my feeling or with and within. So it's always with and within and alongside of."

_____

NEIL DOUGLAS-KLOTZ

THE PRACTICE

Pray in God's Name, in Love's Name.

Whenever you notice that you've prayed while not hearing the Name, the Silence, or the Sound of Silence, stop and start again and hold the intention to hear His Name throughout the entire prayer, knowing that His name, His Word, (t)His Feeling, are more important than your words. Put on the Name of God like a shawl, and don't take It off. Put on the Name, the Silence, and take off words. **Pray without praying, without ceasing.**

"I'm learning to be gentle, to be patient, to not light fires when I cannot see the stars."

_____

WILLIAM BORTZ

How many fires have you set in the past week, in the past two weeks, by trying to run ahead of God, trying to get in front of life, instead of allowing it to unfold?

How does it feel when you're praying?

When you're praying with words?

In John 14:13 (NASB), Jesus said, "Whatever you ask in My Name, this I will do, so that the Father may be glorified in the Son. If you ask Me anything in My name, I will do it."

Later (John 16:24), he said, "Until now you have asked for nothing in My name; ask and you will receive, so that your joy may be made full." You've been asking and asking, maybe even in His Name, the Name you've been taught, the one you've taught, but that's not all He taught. That's not the only Name he taught. The Gospel of Philip says, *"Only one name is not pronounced in the world, the name the Father gave the Son. It is the name above all; it is the Father's name. For the Son would not have become Father if he had not put on the Father's name. Those who have this name understand it but do not speak it. Those who do not have it cannot even understand it."*

Right now, you seemingly do not hear It because there's a wall of thought blocking It,
distracting you from being able to pray in His Name,
to pray in the Presence of the Sound of (t)His Name,
in the awareness of It,
to pray to It,
surrounded by It,
encased in It.
I had that revelation when I was saying the Our Father a couple of years ago.
As I concluded with, "In the Name of the Father and of the Son and the Holy Spirit,"
I could feel It so clearly—

in the Presence of the Name,
of the One that appears as the three,
in the presence of Your Name, God, which is my real Name, I pray.
While hearing Your Name,
I pray.
Amen.

> "Use me, God. Show me how to take who I am, who I want to be and what I can do, and use it for a purpose greater than myself."
>
> OFTEN ATTRIBUTED TO MARTIN LUTHER KING JR.

Can you come into that atmosphere of humility,
which is not a spirit of thinking less of yourself
but thinking about yourself less,
praying for others more than you pray for yourself?
Know that a blessing may come to you because you wished it for
someone else.
Because you stopped thinking about yourself long enough for a
door to open.
That door was closed because you were closed.
It opened because you opened your Awareness beyond yourself,
beyond the world.
A Sufi proverb says, "Humble yourself and you'll grow greater than
the world. Your self will be revealed to you without you."
The Silence will be revealed to you.
His Name is revealed to you.
You can't hear me without also hearing His name.
Just shift your attention from these words to the Silence, and then
listen to the Silence.
What key is the Silence in?

Listen to the Silence like you listen to the hook of your favorite song.

Let the Silence hook you.

It's just as good.

It's even more creative.

It's melodic, but you don't allow yourself to hear.

You keep yourself busy because you're afraid of the Silence.

You're afraid of success.

Once you begin to admit that to yourself,

you admit,

you allow,

you invite the Silence in because you know It is the path.

It is the way.

You can't hear the stars without It.

"We are stars wrapped in skin.

The light you are seeking has always been within." —Anonymous

You can't be the Star you are,

that star wrapped in skin,

without It.

In the beginning,

It's like a little spark,

and then It seems to grow in volume into a flame,

and then into a bonfire,

and then into a star,

zoomed in,

This Son,

the Sound,

bigger,

bolder,

louder.

Your Energy speaks without words.

This Love prays,

It asks without words.

"By silence or stillness is meant in this context not emptiness but fullness, not an absence but a presence. True silence of the heart is an attitude of waiting upon God, of listening to Him, of responding to His love. It is not just the cessation of speech, a pause between words, but rather communion and dialogue. 'This silence,' says Ignatius, 'is at the same time a conversation, yet without thoughts, above every thought.'"

KALLISTOS WARE, FOREWORD TO
IGNATIUS BRIANCHANINOV, *ON THE PRAYER OF JESUS*

Prayer means shedding thought,
shining beyond thought.

"People who shine from within don't need a spotlight."

ATTRIBUTED TO ZIG ZIGLAR

You don't need anything you have,
because now you're praying in His Name.
You're sitting in His Name.
You're breathing in His Name.
You're smiling,
relaxing in His Name.
Until now you've asked for nothing in His name,
but it's a new dawn.

"Once dust, you're now Spirit.
Once ignorant, now wise.
He who has led you this far will guide you further.
The momentum is in place.
The river is moving.
The charge is alive,
this constant unfolding.
Stay with it,
stay in it."

———————

UNKNOWN

Stay as the Name.
Your whole life appears to be happening in the Name.
That's all you have to do, listen for It while you're working,
while you're resting,
while you're praying.
If you prayed while not hearing the Name,
stop and start again and hold the intention to hear His name
throughout the entire prayer,
knowing that it's His name,
His word, that's more important than your words.
His plan is bigger than your plan.
There's no delay.
Everything in time is right on time,
but you're beyond time,
infinitely patient,
seeing without eyes,
hearing without ears.
His Name saved you, and It is saving you.

You are now being (Y)our highest vibration.
Keep it on.

Affirm: I Am a Star
What sound does a Star make?
Ask yourself this question and listen to the Silence that follows.
Every time you're noticing thoughts today and this week,
pause,
and come back Here.
To the Scintillating-Silence.
Hear your Light.
Feel your Light.
When you dissolve thoughts in this Light, you're dissolving the
problem.
Whatever it was you were thinking about is also clearing—
the sky of your mind is clearing,
revealing the twinkling Star,
the Sun, the Son
that you are,
that I Am.
Note: This Scintillating-Silence is not just in your head, between
your ears. It's everywhere. Your whole being is This. You are a
Star. The Sun. The Son. This Light that you can't help but give
off is felt and heard by You. This Love that you can't help but
share is Your Gift. Your God-given talent is to shine, to glow, to
be Him in your home today, on the highway today, at your office
all week. Even if your Silence isn't sounding, just hear the
Silence. Be the Silence. It is enough. You'll have more than
enough if you live in this place. You'll be protected if you live in
this place, aware of the Word. Meditating on It, receiving It,
embracing It, knowing that It is appearing as you.

How to Become Like a Child in the Kingdom

Pause in the midst of a familiar train of thought about who or what is bothering you. Scan your body.

Let go of the tension you find.

Letting go of the tension on the inside is the healing.

You'll begin to experience a constant,

conscious Peace inside,

and harmony outside, until you see that there is no inside and outside.

Only Peace. Only Harmony, Only this Love.

REMEMBER:

Feeling Love is the letting go.

When you keep feeling Love, you keep letting go into Love.

And when only Love is left, what appears can only be in the image of that Love. You realize life is really GoOD.

THE QUOTE

"Jesus said, 'The kingdom of heaven is within you.' . . . I think if he lived nowadays, instead of 'kingdom,' he would have said, 'dimension.' And 'heaven' refers to a sense of vastness or spaciousness. So if we retranslate the words of Jesus into modern terms, [it would be] 'the dimension of spaciousness is within you.'"

———————

ECKHART TOLLE

THE PRACTICE

If you're going to be that human today, be like a child.
Close that body's eyes and find that Dimension of Spaciousness.
Not within that body, but within Consciousness.
Recognize that It's already always the case.
It's right there.
It's not even buried under your thoughts.
It's not even buried under strong emotions.
It's not even veiled by them or eclipsed by anger or fear.
This loving, quiet still point and boundless expanse is here.
When you're aware of It,
the thoughts slow down and it's much easier to recognize the Dimension of Spaciousness.
It's always there, even when the thoughts are loud.
But in the beginning we practice,
slipping in between the thoughts,
hanging out in the gaps,
until we become so familiar with this Dimension of Spaciousness
that the conditions don't matter.
The inner conditions don't matter.
The outer conditions don't matter.
We can't help but remember This.

We can't help but be This.
In the Bible (Matthew 18:3), we're told that we can't enter the
Kingdom unless we become like little children.
Knowing what you know now,
feeling what you feel now,
what do you think that very famous Bible quote means,
unless you become like little children?

Sri Ramana Maharshi said, "A child and a Sage are similar in a way. Incidents interest a child only so long as they last. It ceases to think of them after they have passed away. So then, it is apparent that they do not leave any impression on the child and it is not affected by them mentally. So it is with a Sage." And so it is with you. To be like a child means that when anything comes up that seems to cause a disturbance within, you recognize it and use it as an invitation to return to your Dimension of Spaciousness. And from there, you deal with the disturbance. And oftentimes, you'll find the problem isn't there. When you return to that Dimension of Spaciousness, that problem can't even exist on that level.

> "Whatever happened, had to happen. Don't sit and think 'I could have done this or that.' It is of no use. Leave your burden, clear the mind, and move on."
>
> ———
>
> **SRI SRI RAVI SHANKAR**

And so when any old, tired, rerun train of thought comes up for you today, and this week, don't go down that rabbit hole. Become aware of that train of thought and use it as an invitation to return to Love, to this felt-Peace, this Oneness, and stay (t)here. Abide there. And then you'll watch your attention drift back into those types of thoughts, and then you'll watch attention return to this Dimension of Spaciousness, to the Stillness that you can relax even more into right now.

Breathe into right now.
Breathe into your Heart.
Let your shoulders melt.
Feel the Love that surrounds you.
Feel the Love that you are that surrounds that body.
Feel the Spaciousness that surrounds that body.
Feel the Space that that body is seated in.
You are that space.
You are that Dimension of Spaciousness.
It is You.
And from there, as you watch what you thought You were,
try to remember This.
Try to understand This.
Try to practice this,
sometimes successfully,
sometimes failing.
But the Spaciousness that You are,
the spaciousness that I Am,
it's not affected by any of this.

If you're going to be that human today, be like a child. Let stuff go. Immediately return to Love. Alternatively, you can practice being what you are already, this Kingdom that you are. Stay here as this Kingdom and your world experience will be that of a king, fully protected so that you can protect and heal others while simultaneously knowing that nothing has ever happened.

Inner Silence means you're in the Kingdom.

"Until you know Truth you can't quiet the mind. That is the anesthetic for the mind, Truth. And so that is the area that must be strengthened for an individual who finds that I still cannot be still. You do not know the Truth yet. You do not even know the letter of Truth at this point, because with the letter of Truth in consciousness, that provides the peace that in turn opens the way for the inspiration."

HERB FITCH

Those Aren't Your Problems; They're Mine

It's like a switch gets flipped from my seeing my thirteen-year-old,
to feeling the Christ where I see my thirteen-year-old.
It happens just that fast.
But it's not me.
God is remembering in me,
God is pulling the veil back, like,
"See, that's not your child, she's Mine;
that's not your house, that's Mine;
these aren't your problems, they're Mine;
that's not your health, not your body; it's Mine.
That's not you breathing; that's Me."
And the weight gets lifted,
and the Silence gets louder,
and the Love gets stronger,
and there's only Gratitude.

THE QUOTES

"All I know is Love, and I find my heart infinite and everywhere."

———————

"The giving and receiving is the tricky thing. It's not the gift. It's what the heart says in giving the gift, and from my point of view, one doesn't give or receive—that's a role we have to play. But the gift—it's God's gift. I think that it's better to be souls than roles."

———————

RAM DASS

THE PRACTICE

Leave your roles today. Be Soul.

The Indian spiritual teacher and yogi Swami Satchidananda said, "The flower doesn't know it is giving fragrance. Does it even say, 'I want to give a nice smell. Here is a nice person. I want to be extra nice to him'? A candle doesn't know it is giving light. It doesn't worry you, 'Look. I'm wasting my time; I'm melting away. Come and read something with my light.' Does the candle ask you that?"

No, the candle is just sitting there,
just like you right now.
Just your very presence.
And people enjoy the light of God,
the fragrance of God.

> "People get the benefit of God just by your being, by your remembering who you are. That's your gift. That's your power."
>
> UNKNOWN

Then enjoy your Heart.
Not the physical one.
This One isn't something that can be operated on.
It's not something that can be understood with the mind.
It's not located in a specific place on the left-side center of that chest,
or spiritually, invisibly, on the right side,
but these can be used as a doorway to the true Heart and to the
spiritual one that is everywhere.

Everywhere you look,
you see your Heart.
You feel your Heart.
You see a person,
but you feel your Heart.

It's easy for me to remember to do this when I'm in public around "strangers," seemingly, on the street, to look at the direction of people and feel my Heart.

But when I'm at home, it's more of a challenge to remember this practice because I'm so into the "mommy" role.

"Make sure you do your homework."

"Go double-check that math homework, please."

"Help me do this."

"Thank you for doing that."

It's very mommy/daughter, mommy/son.

But when I'm consciously remembering to transcend roles,
the stuff still gets done,
but there's less stress.
There's less tension,
more ease,
more Love.
When it's bedtime,
it's easy to remember,
but I've been actively practicing during the day, on the fly.

"God's activities are so subtle, and simultaneously so profound, that the mind is blind to them, but not the heart."

UNKNOWN

Stay out of roles today by being aware of them.
Stay in your Heart today.
Stay in His heart.
Be that Heart today.
The Love in every room,
the Love between that body that's sitting there contemplating this
and the other bodies that live in that house or work in that office.
You are the love between them. That's what Nisargadatta Maharaj
said—

"In marriage you are neither the husband nor the wife; you
are the love between the two."

You could also say you're the Love appearing as them
and the Love between them,
pervading them,
surrounding them.
The words don't matter.
They're just entry points to get you to the experience of This.
Not thinking, "All I know is Love,"
not thinking, "My heart is infinite and everywhere,"
but experiencing that.
Only Love.
I Am the Heart.
I Am Everywhere.
It's not that I see Nikki everywhere.
I practiced feeling Love here, where Nikki appears to be,
until it was obvious that this Love wasn't just here;
It's everywhere,
and It is myself.
And so now,
wherever Nikki looks,
wherever the gaze falls,
Love is felt.
The whole room, the scene, in the feeling of Love.
I feel Love while I look at the room.
I feel Love while I look at the people.
I look at them Lovingly.
I don't let any sight, any appearance, anything, overshadow this
Loving feeling.
I don't let any thought distract me from this Love.

I cannot stress this practice enough. If all you can hear is the Silence when you turn within, that's perfect. The Love will announce itself in that quiet, as that Quiet. But until then, just hear the Silence.

That Silence right (t)Here.

And don't forget to hear It while you're looking, while you're thinking, while you're tasting, touching, smelling, while you're hearing noise, while you're hearing music, be the Silence. That's all you have to do, is be. Just be.

"As for the Word—
his wisdom meditates on it,
his teaching utters it,
his knowledge has revealed it,
his patience is a crown upon it,
his joy is in harmony with it,
his glory has exalted it,
his character has revealed it,
his rest has received it,
his love has incarnated it,
his faith has embraced it."

"THE FATHER UTTERS THE NAMES OF PEOPLE WHO KNOW,"
THE GOSPEL OF TRUTH, *THE NAG HAMMADI SCRIPTURES*

Loving Is the Reaping

As you read these words, listen for your heart beating.
And as you read this line, become aware of your breath.
And as you read this line, become aware of Love,
no matter how subtle,
no matter how light,
in your hands, in your feet, in your chest.
You're feeling The Password right now.
I'm sharing It with you right now.
But It's not a word.
It's a feeling. A GoOD one.
And when you're aware of It, you gain access to the eternal Silence
beyond the heart beating,
to the blissful Stillness beyond the breath,
to the Love beyond thoughts.
Give this Password to every inner and outer barrier today.
Feel Love.
And go beyond.

THE QUOTES

"I carry light and silence."

_____

ANNA SWIR

"Unless you give up the idea that the world is real, your mind will always be after it."

SRI RAMANA MAHARSHI

"You need not aspire for or get any new state. Get rid of your present thoughts, that is all."

SRI RAMANA MAHARSHI

THE PRACTICE:

Affirm: "I carry Light and Silence."
I keep my eye on the feeling of Love,
and this eye doesn't blink,
It doesn't lose sight of this Feeling beyond feelings,
of this Faith beyond appearances.
It's opened.
And It opens.
It's blessed.
and It blesses.
Loving is the Reaping.
Place your hand over your heart,
and call out for God.
But let the call come from your Heart.
Not your mind,
not your mouth,
not up there in your head.
Drop down,
and call with this feeling of Love constantly.
And then stop all "doing" and be.
It's impossible to go any further without attention on this Love.

Until your attention becomes Love.
That's why the doors appear to be closed.
Why the roads appear to be blocked.
Why it appears to be dark.
Close your eyes and invite God in.
"God, come into my life.
Be here with me.
Pray here,
Your prayer of Silence, in me.
I carry Your Light as Silence."

Affirm, "I carry Light and Silence," as you rock back and forth, as if imitating walking or motion, practicing staying aware of this Light and Silence. Even when that body is moving, I carry Light and Silence. I carry Light in Silence, I carry Light as Silence.

These are just words, easy to get lost in, easy to play with, to rearrange, to manipulate, but there's something here beyond them. And even though these words don't make sense, it's the only way I can share. It's like I keep my eye on the feeling of love and this eye doesn't blink. It doesn't lose sight of this feeling that's beyond all feelings. I'm aware of this. Even when Nikki is angry, this is still there. Even when she's scared.

The Indian spiritual teacher Mother Meera said, "The final reality is the Light and Love of God." She said, "Root yourself in that final reality always and at every moment, and evil will crumble around you."

Believing we are human beings rather than Spirit Being is the evil itself. Believing we are human rather than spiritual is the disease itself. It's the lack itself, as Joel Goldsmith says. And you don't have to believe differently; you just have to be silent. In the silence, there are no beliefs. There is no evil. There is no disease. There is no lack. There is no you. There's only This.

Recall that Sri Ramana Maharshi said, "Unless you give up the idea that the world is real, your mind will always be after it" and "You need not aspire for or get any new state. Get rid of your present thoughts, that is all." That is Light as Silence.

> "Is a lamp brought in to be placed under a bushel basket or under a bed, and not to be placed on a lampstand? For there is nothing hidden except to be made visible; nothing is secret except to come to light."
>
> ———
>
> **JESUS (MARK 4:21-23)**

Just above your head is a Flame.
The Flame of Truth,
Attention,
and Love.
The Flame of the Holy Spirit.
You carry It everywhere you go,
enlightening every room,
space,
and heart before you can even speak a word.
You're becoming conscious of this Light you wear like a crown,
like the halo you see depicted in holy icons.
Your time in hiding has come to an end.
Feeling Love is the uncovering.
The revealing.
The reaping.

You Are Shelter(ed)

THE QUOTES

"Christhood is our true identity, not good humanhood, not bad humanhood."

———————

JOEL GOLDSMITH, *THE MYSTICAL I*

THE PRACTICE

Affirm: "Not good humanhood, not bad humanhood;
invisible Christhood."
Love is the complete reality, and I Am that Love.
Every time thoughts come as to how it's going to happen,
when it's going to happen,
close that body's eyes . . .
fold its hands in front of it,
and go back down into that bowing,
back into that Humbleness.
Bow back into God,
back into your Shelter,
like you're ducking under the doorframe back inside,
where it's quiet,

where there is no world, nothing to solve, nothing to fix, nothing to
think about.
That's the point.
Not good humanhood, not bad humanhood, Christhood.
Make that your mantra this week,
and when you're saying it,
you're unseeing good people,
you're unseeing bad people,
you're unseeing you, the "person" you think you are,
you're unseeing all the people,
all the world.
Only Christhood is here,
which means only this Loving Silence is here,
and you feel that Loving Silence
you BE that Loving Silence,
Only,
Formless,
Silent,
and that heals,
that feeds,
that pays,
that's Love,
that's All.

Use that body as an antenna again, and fold its hands in front of it in prayer, and bow its head. Notice how different you are, how different you feel, in this posture. Close that body's eyes and notice that you are now in the shelter of Silence. You are surrounded by Silence.

Even if there is noise where you are, it's outside of the shelter of Silence. It can't touch the Shelter. My words don't touch your Shelter. Your thoughts can't touch (t)His Shelter. You hear everything, but you hear the Silence first. You hear the Silence loudest.

Dr. Bruce Davis said, "Every noise you hear, you are given to heal." To turn back into Silence, to recognize that it, too, is Silence, even while it's sounding. Even while you're hearing it, you're knowing that you're hearing only Silence. And you thank that Silence without using words, for that Peace you're beginning to feel.

> "To completely trust in God is to be like a child who knows deeply that even if he does not call for the mother, the mother is totally aware of his condition and is looking after him."
>
> ABU HAMID MUHAMMAD AL-GHAZALI

This shelter you're in, God is in. The Spirit of God is in that room, in that car, in that Silence, that Shelter you are, and that body. And the appearance of that body is God. And just as you don't have to tell yourself, "I am hungry"; you just go eat, you don't have to tell Him what you need; He just provides. You just have to keep quiet like this.

> "'Quiet' doesn't mean that a person should sit like a statue. 'Peace' means that there should be no concept or thought in mind. If thought arises in the mind, time will also arise. When the thought that produces time vanishes time also ceases to exist. Then there is true peace. Anyone can try this. Keep quiet for a single instant. Don't allow the mind to stir. For a single moment be without any thought of the past. In that moment you will see that there is no thought, no time, no world. This is what I mean by peace. In that instant everything will be peaceful. If you keep quiet you will see that the whole world is quiet.

"This world does not exist at all. If you sit quietly for a single
second you will bring peace to the world because in that moment
there is no world. Then do it for the next second, and the next.
This [is] the way to bring about peace, but you have to do it
yourself and see."

PAPAJI H. W. L. POONJA

Keep noticing your breath like this.
And then you go that next step further and recognize that which is
not breathing.
That the awareness of the breathing is not breathing,
The awareness of that heart beating is not pulsating,
it's not moving,
it's not sounding.
It doesn't take breaks.
That's why it's hard getting back into the swing of things after the
weekend,
after vacation,
after a break.
But as long as you stay home in the Shelter,
even as you go out and about and do the things,
it's like it's still the Sabbath.
You're still resting.
As long as you're hearing, you're blessing,
you're being a blessing in those places where you feel like you
don't want to be,
you're not choosing to be,
but you have to be.
Remember that this isn't mundane.

You're not here by chance.
You're here because God wants you to be.
You couldn't be anywhere else, or else you would be.
There's an old Sufi saying that goes,

"To get what you love, you must first be patient with what
you hate."

That's been my experience. Finding and feeling Love in that place where it feels impossible, or with that person where it feels impossible, that is your only purpose in that room, in that building, in that situation: to notice that you are Sheltered. And you can hear the Silence, even though you hear them. The moment you can do that, I promise you, things will begin to change. Things shift. People leave. They get fired, they move on. You get hired somewhere else, promoted here. Business plan there, new opportunities. You don't know how it'll play out. That's not your business, at least not on this level. You just abide here and trust.

Every time thoughts come as to how it's going to happen, when it's going to happen, close that body's eyes and know that everything has already happened. It's like you're trying to fast-forward the movie. Trust that the plot will be suspenseful and entertaining; trust that the ending will be happy. Trust that you can watch again (we call that déjà vu). Trust that there will be a sequel. "Trust," which means watch silently. Thoughtlessly.

You Are What You're Seeking

THE QUOTES

"Seek the Father behind all fathers
And the Mother behind all mothers."

———————

YOGANANDA PARAMHANSA, *THE DIVINE ROMANCE*

Seek the only Beloved behind all loved ones
And the friend behind all friends
Of many lives lived on this mystery-earth.
Search for the Brain behind all brains
And the Mind behind all minds,
The Hand behind all hands
And the Feet behind all feet.
Seek the Blood behind all bloods,
The Breath behind all breaths,
The Wisdom behind all wisdom
And the Joy behind all joys.
Find the Love behind all loves,
The Life behind all living things.

"Divine love is the magnet that draws to me all good."

_____

PARAMHANSA YOGANANADA

"You are a magnet. Not a claw."

_____

UNKNOWN

THE PRACTICE

Every time you catch yourself seeking something or someone, seek the Love. As soon as It's sought, It's found as You. When you're feeling Love, you're being Love.

Seeking the Silence behind your thoughts, this week,
and the Love behind your body,
you arrive at your Self.
When you seek the Eternal Day behind "Monday,"
the Timelessness behind time,
you arrive at your Self.
Nothing can touch you here.
No one can "block" you here,
because there's nothing but You here.
There's nothing but Love here,
and this Divine Love is presently, right now as you're reading these
words, becoming all the
GoOD things you need. Watch:
Nothing is holding you back.
No one is holding you back.
You're not unwanted or unloved.
You're not lacking anything.
These are just thoughts that you've been believing in and giving

your attention to for years.
Those same thoughts come here.
Those same thoughts come to every seeming one.
They're not your thoughts.
They're not my thoughts.
They're not their thoughts.
They're just thoughts.
They're not even there, really.
But when you claim them as your own,
when you cling to them and hold on to them,
repeat them,
own them like the thought, "Monday sucks."
That's when you suffer, then Monday does suck.
What's behind the thought, "Monday sucks"?
What's just in back of it?
What's right next to it?
What's pervading it?
What sees it?
What sees the thought Mondays suck?

I receive a lot of messages from listeners who feel enlightenment is out of reach and they feel inspired and sometimes very clear, but at other times they feel blocked. They feel like they can't feel this Love.

What's behind the thought, "I can't feel Love"? Look past that thought. Jump off that thought and onto the Silence that's right there, behind that thought and every thought.

The same silence you're listening to now. The Silence of Space, of the Cosmos, of God. The same Silence that is Love. Yogananda said, "This divine love is like a magnet that draws to you all your good, an all-powerful magnet," one that can't be blocked.

Close that body's eyes and be the magnet that you are.
Be still,
be silent.
Magnets aren't thinking about being magnets.
They're not doubting or questioning their magnetic power,
their ability to attract.
They're just being themselves.
When you're feeling Love,
you're being your Self,
drawing everything to you that you need effortlessly,
silently,
powerfully.
Let this Love organize Itself.
Allow it to take shape all around you.
Don't try to imagine the forms.
Look past that imagining to the stillness.
Go back to feeling Love.
Stay with the Love,
not even with good thoughts.
Dissolve every thought,
even visualizations of what you want in the future.
Of that is promised you in the future (don't worry, it's here).
Dissolve it.
Trust the Love to take its destined shape.
Trust that as long as you're being yourself,
what's meant for you is drawn to you.
It's law.

Can you feel this Power you are?
How attractive you are.
You're smiling now.
That mind is silent because it's focused on the Silence now.
It's focused on God now instead of problems,
instead of thoughts that don't belong to you.
In the Silent Love,

you'll find everything including love for Mondays because you're not focused on the concept of Monday, the idea, the thought of Monday. You're focused on what's behind it. The eternal day behind the day. The timelessness behind the time. The Love behind that body, the Love that is appearing as that body. Focus on that today. I'm focusing in and on, and as that same place. We share that place.

In this Place there's only One of us.

The Unreal Cannot Overwhelm the Real (How to Stop Feeling Overwhelmed)

THE QUOTE

"God is in me. God is with me. God is for me."

———————

SARDINE BREAD (@SARDINEBREAD ON INSTAGRAM)

THE PRACTICE

Affirm: "The Presence is on me, in me, for me."
And then just do it. Don't think about it. Just do it. Just watch it
accomplish everything.
Just as "a movie can't overwhelm the screen," (Rupert Spira,
from an online talk)
no moment, no thought, no emotion—no matter the intensity—
can overwhelm this Love you are.
Yes, change is hard.
And yes, change is Here.
This "challenge" is how the miracle you've been asking for,
waiting for,
looking for,

begins.
Just keep walking.
As long as you're feeling Love,
know you're going the right way.
This is your sign.
God has sent (t)His Love
for us to follow
out of the illusion.
So don't let anything distract you from this Love.
Not yourself,
not your thoughts,
or anyone else.
Nothing is worth it.
Nothing, this No Thing, this Silence, is worth it.
It's worth your attention.
It made you worthy.
It made you Holy.
It has given you a Purpose.
And right now, It looks like whatever you are called to do "today."
The pressure is not on you,
the Presence is on you.

On February 3, 2003, a Friday, I woke up before my alarm, at least an hour before my alarm. I didn't know the exact time because my eyes were still closed and I was aware of so many thoughts about the day ahead, about the next day. It was to be my first busy weekend of the year. I try to reserve my weekends for rest, but that cannot always happen.

My son was turning six on the following Monday, so there was a birthday party. My daughter's friend was also having a birthday party. My son needed a haircut. I had a dentist appointment later that day. There were business meetings and a concert, and I could feel the tension. I could feel the heart beating faster than it should have been beating while resting in the bed, and then I remembered what my Grandma Maxine used to say, what she used to tell my mom and what my mom reminds me of all the time now: "Just do it. Just do it. Don't think about it. You just do it."

You get up and you do it, and it doesn't feel as heavy as it felt when you were thinking about it, when it wasn't here yet. When it's here, you can handle it. When it's here, you live it no matter what it is. Seemingly good or bad. I'm sure you can remember intense moments, emergency moments, where if you had known it was coming, you would've been sick with thoughts about how you would handle it, how you couldn't handle it, but when it was happening, when that's what was, it was just another moment.

Let your mind be stilled by this power.
That's what I did this morning.
I lay there, aware of thoughts,
aware of the worry,
using the thoughts and the worry to point me back here.
The thoughts and the worry used to pull me out there into the world,
but now,
as soon as I become aware of them,
they're like signposts that point me back here,
that keep me,
hold me, here.
It feels effortful at first for the mind to hold the silence,
to not take a step to the right or to the left,
but to stay right here in the quiet.
Every time a thought comes and pulls at you,
tugs your arm,
you pull it back and you abide.
And you don't have to do this for long.
Just see if you can make it two minutes not following the thoughts.
A thought will come during that two minutes,
 but your practice is to see if you can stay as the silence.

There's a difference between "I won't have thoughts for two minutes" and "I will have thoughts, but I won't follow them. I won't think about the thoughts. I'll become aware of a thought and then I'll hear this and then I'll stay here."

I play the quiet game with my kids all the time. Play that game, but no silent words or movements are allowed either. Don't blink, and see that you also won't think.

Remember, Sri Ramana Maharshi said, "Unless you give up the idea that the world is real, your mind will always be after it." That's why the mantra "Only Love is here" or "Only God is here" or "Only Silence is here," or "Not good humanhood, not bad humanhood, Invisible Christhood," works. This invisible, all-pervading Presence, that's all that's here. That's why those pointers are so powerful, because for those moments, you are no longer thinking "This problem is real. This thing is important. I'm so stressed. I've got so much to do." For those brief moments, you're seeing through, you're seeing beyond. You're being beyond. God has sent this Love for us to follow out of the illusion. Like a rope or a bread-crumb trail.

You left It for yourself.
Feel It with me now.
When I'm feeling It,
It makes me rock.
It makes me sway.
It makes me smile.
It holds my mind until it melts.
Last week, while in meditation,
a white heart appeared.
It didn't have sharp edges,
but it was clearly heart-shaped, this light, and then it

turned purple,

like a royal purple,

and then it was as if it melted and that purple substance
went everywhere.

It was so vivid that I opened my eyes shortly after and Googled "purple hearts Christ," "purple hearts Krishna," just to see if there was anything, as if Google had the answers to everything.

And there were actually quite a few things about Jesus and purple hearts, but what was interesting was when I pulled back up to the house after picking my kids up from school. After talking and singing and laughing, and probably playing the silent game a little, too (my favorite game!), before we got out of the car, my son says, "Oh, mom, I need to give you something. I got these from school. Two purple hearts."

I'm telling this story because there was something about that melting, how that substance, that essence, was seen to be everywhere. Like it says in the Gospel of Thomas, "The Father's kingdom is spread out upon the earth, and people do not see it." It made me think about when someone asked Maharajji about how the Christ meditated and they said it seemed as if he was about to answer, but instead his eyes closed and he sat there completely still, completely silent.

It felt like he totally disappeared. Krishna Das wrote, "In all the time I'd been with him, I'd only seen him sitting motionless like this a couple of times before. It was extraordinarily powerful, as if the whole universe had become silent. Then a tear came down his cheek. We were in awe. After a couple of minutes, his eyes half opened and, with great emotion, he quietly said, 'He lost himself in love, that's how he meditated. He was one with all beings. He loved everyone, even the people who crucified him. He never died. He is the atman [soul]. He lives in the hearts of all.'"

I hadn't thought of that quote until now. I didn't know what that meditation meant until now. That's why I say this is my practice and I'm thankful that you practice with me. I'm with you here in the Silence. Every time you hear the Silence, I'm with you. It makes me think of those old-school movies where friends are separated by distance, but they're both looking out their window at the same moon. We're hearing the same Silence. We're feeling the same Love.

As frequently as you can remember to this week, give yourself permission to pause the overwhelm so you can hear God playing, Joy dancing, Silence singing. Whenever the "busy mom" or "busy dad" train of thoughts starts, STOP, listen again for the train of Silence, and then do the things from (t)here. Don't get ahead of your Self; that's all "overwhelm" is. Notice how often you're trying to be one step ahead of God, one step ahead of your story. Breathe. Let Love unfold. Let Love do it through you. And watch everything get done.

> "Nature does not hurry, yet everything is accomplished."
>
> ———
>
> LAO TZU

Your roots meet me in the Nothingness.
If you can feel your roots,
you can feel me.
If we can feel our roots,
we can feel God.
We're being nourished by God,
enlivened by God,
breathed by God,
prospered by God.
Overwhelmed by God.
God is You.

Retire That Old Prayer

You keep trying the same key,
But this is a new door.
You keep praying the same prayer,
wanting the same thing,
but to receive it,
you have to let it go.
You have to pick up His Name,
the Sound of Silence,
the Love.
Don't worry.
What's coming through you will be in time.

THE QUOTE

"Our whole purpose is to lead people to the realization of God's omnipresence and their constant availability; to speak to Him without thought or words: humility is enough to sit down (or even stand or lie down), close your eyes and recognize:

"'I of myself, can do nothing. The Father in me is the One who does the works. Speak, Lord, that your son listens.'

"Then wait a minute or two in expectant silence before getting up and continuing the tasks."

_____

JOEL GOLDSMITH, *A LESSON TO SAM*

THE PRACTICE

Retire that old prayer by retiring yourself. You're not a person. You're Vibration. You're Spirit. You're Love. *The moment you ask for help, you are again a person with problems.*

Something's bothering you.

Drop it here in the Silence.

Speak it into the Silence and leave it here with Me,

the way you throw a penny in a wishing well, in a fountain.

Sri Sri Ravi Shankar said that's why they were invented. Our ancestors knew that when a desire comes, you drop it; immediately, you drop it. That's how it comes to you, not by holding it. But many people now, they leave the penny but they keep the thought. They keep the prayer. They keep the desire. They keep the trouble.

What's troubling you?

Drop it into the silence.

Speak it one last time.

Think it one last time and then leave it here.

"Whenever I feel helpless in this overwhelming world, I become a helper. During the times when it feels like I have no power, I serve others. Whenever I help wash the world's feet, my hands stop shaking. And I know peace."

_____

JOHN ROEDEL (@JOHN_ROEDEL_WRITER ON INSTAGRAM)

You're no longer afraid, shaking, worrying. You're still. And in the stillness, you can close that body's eyes and recognize, "I of myself can do nothing. The Father in me is the one who does the works. Speak, Lord. Your servant heareth." And then, like Joel Goldsmith said, you "wait a minute or two in expectant silence" and then get up and go about your day. It's a new way of solving problems. Sometimes the problems resolve spontaneously. Sometimes they resolve in seeming steps that are revealed to you, but this initiates it.

Knowing you don't need a solution initiates a healing.

> **"When you know it doesn't exist. Then it appears."**
>
> ———————
>
> **HERB FITCH**

Another powerful pointer is to use a prayer said to have originated with Mother Teresa. If you feel distressed during your day, call upon Our Lady: "Mary, mother of Jesus, please be a mother to me now."

"Please be a mother to me now." Say those words and notice where they leave you.

They leave you where God can find you. In the Silence, in this Love, in this Humbleness. Where the only desire is for this uninterrupted Love.

When no desires remain, you revert to your natural state. You are Silence appearing as everything. Once a desire is fulfilled, you're back where you started, right here in the Silence.

"But Nikki, if I stay in the silence, won't I just give up? Won't I forget my desires or not care if they come or not? Maybe they'll miss me. Maybe God will miss me altogether."

Ram Dass said: "The most exquisite paradox. As soon as you give it all up, you can have it all. How about that one? As long as you want power, you can't have it. The minute you don't want power, you'll have more than you ever dreamed possible."

You have everything you need already. It doesn't look like it. Your eyes deceive you. Your mind is misleading. You don't believe it. You're not lacking anything. You're not late to anything. You haven't missed a thing except This. The Silence, this Love, was the only thing you were missing. It's the key that opens that door. A door that's not really there. It's the Christ that lives within you, but not "you," that body that looks back at you in the mirror. That's not you. You can't be seen with eyes. No one can see you, not the real you. But I can feel you. I feel what's coming through you, so stop worrying. Drop the worry. It'll be in time.

When a desire comes, or the impulse to check in on a prayer that was already prayed is perceived, I immediately drop my shoulders back down (I notice they come up when thought is present; the jaw is also clenched sometimes) and feel into the space next to the desire. It's a subtle shift back into the Silent-Love. You could say I become aware of the desire, and that triggers me to turn to Love.

What do you hear when thinking stops?
When wanting stops?
Ask yourself that question, and linger in the silence behind the question.
Who am I when I want nothing?
Before I went to India for the third time (April 2024),
I was told in a very Divine way, by a very Divine Friend—
Gudu—
to go there with an empty heart,
and an empty mind,
not wanting anything,
not desiring anything,
not craving anything,

not seeking solutions or answers,
not seeking anything,
not expecting anything at all.
And I felt it.
I heard that message so clearly.
And of course, the mind came up, and I asked, "Well, how do I
do that? How do I go about doing that?"
And Gudu said, "Just Love God."
The Loving replaces the wanting.
It eclipses it.
You just keep quiet.
You go where there are no words,
and you find the Love (t)here,
and you place your attention (t)here.
The wanting may still be (t)here,
but your attention is on the Loving;
it's on the having.
He said, "You come like that,
you come empty and open,
and you'll get everything you want.
Everything you wanted.
That's the secret."

Listen with Your Eyes

THE QUOTE

"If the Beautiful One is not hidden inside you, then what is that Light hidden under your cloak?"

———————

RUMI

THE PRACTICE

Affirm: "'I Am' is my Power.
'I Am' is the only Power.
All I have to do is hear It,
is feel It,
is be It,
and the earth melts (it's seen as not truly real),
and the miracle happens."
"What is that light you're beginning to feel before you even have to reach for it?"
Rumi said, "Listen with your eyes";
this isn't a Light you can see.
It's one you see with,
and this Light can hear Itself.
It's hearing Itself.
You can hear your Self between my words,

between those thoughts.
With practice,
you never stop hearing your Self.
You never stop hearing God's voice, no matter the environment that
body appears to be in.
No matter how upset or how excited that body appears to be,
you come to realize there's no end,
no interruption, in this Light.
The Silence is unbroken,
and It's the answer to every question,
to every problem,
to every doubt,
to every need.

Close your eyes and remember what you're looking at,
who you're looking at.
Zora Neale Hurston said, "They seemed to be staring at the dark,
but their eyes were watching God."
Where we perceive this darkness,
God is.
What we are perceiving this darkness with
is God.
Bow to It,
to this Presence.
Hold your hands in front of you and lower your head,
and immediately feel Its Love.
Feel Its invisible Hand on you,
on your life,
on your relationships,
on your projects,
on that future you can't see but you're feeling,
the GoODness of It,

the promise of It.
You're affirming It silently,
not with words,
not with limitations of your past,
of what you think is possible.
Just this quiet acknowledgement of God where you are,
of God with us.
That's the seeming first step on this pathless path to enlightenment.
Sri Ramana Maharshi said,

"There is a stage in the beginning, when you identify yourself with the body, when you are still having the body-consciousness. At that stage, you have the feeling you are different from the reality [of] God, and then it is, you think of yourself as a devotee of God or as a servant or lover of God. This is the first stage. The second stage is when you think of yourself as a spark of the divine fire or a ray from the divine Sun. Even then there is still that sense of difference and the body-consciousness. The third stage will come when all such difference ceases to exist, and you realise that the Self alone exists. There is an 'I' which comes and goes, and another 'I' which always exists and abides. So long as the first 'I' exists, the body-consciousness and the sense of diversity . . . will persist. Only when that 'I' dies, the reality will reveal itself."

The Silence is the reality. You don't need answers. You need Silence. Thankfully, since you are It, you don't need It. You just need to become aware of It. In the moment an upset arises, in the moment a problem appears, in the moment a need makes itself known, you're not fooled. You're not tempted to think. You immediately hear. You immediately come back Here and you hear, you listen.

> "In the stillness of the quiet, if we listen, we can hear
> the whisper of the heart giving strength to weakness,
> courage to fear, hope to despair."
>
> ———————
>
> HOWARD THURMAN

The Silence is giving sanctuary.
It's giving security.
It's giving certainty where doubt appears to be.
It's giving God where you appear to be.
Can you look through this book,
through these words,
through that space you appear to be in?
Can you listen with your eyes?
When I'm listening with my eyes,
I'm not blinking.
When I'm listening with my eyes,
I'm feeling Love and hearing Silence.
What I see doesn't change,
but while I see it,
I simultaneously know that it's not there truly,
that this body isn't here truly.
That Nikki isn't here truly.
That these words aren't here truly.
That these thoughts aren't here truly.
This mood or this emotion isn't here truly.
Only God is here, truly.
That whole understanding happens in an instant. It's not verbal,
it's not mental. It just is. It's what I Am.
Mooji said,

"If I, the feeling, the true 'I am' is identified with the body and the person, then it will be the person's responsibility to look after their own life. But if the 'I' is identified as consciousness, then it will be the consciousness that looks after the body. This is the joy of the surrendered ones."

The Joy that is shining through you right now, that has risen in your heart again, that is smiling your face again, that is breathing you softly and confidently and powerfully. You're back in your power.

You Have to Be Mother Now

THE QUOTES

"Jesus said, 'What you will hear in your ear, in the other ear proclaim from your rooftops. For no one lights a lamp and puts it under a basket, nor does one put it in a hidden place. Rather, one puts it on a stand so that all who come and go will see its light.'"

———————

ABBOT GEORGE BURKE, *THE GOSPEL OF THOMAS FOR AWAKENING*

"Whatever you can become is not what you are."

———————

BENJAMIN RAMAKRISHNA (@THEHAMSTERWHEELISNOTMOTORIZED ON INSTAGRAM)

THE PRACTICE

To get to the GoOD part of your life,
you have to die to this part.
You have to not react to this part,
not desire or want in this part.
You have to be Baba now.
You have to be Christ now.
You have to be Mother now.
You aren't becoming.

You aren't believing.
You're be-Loving.

> "[Jesus said,] God spoke the word and I appeared, not of my own or another's volition, but I was sent forth by the Father as a living witness that life is good, for God is good."
>
> ———
>
> **VIRGINIA STEPHENSON**

You have to see as the Christ does.
Close that body's eyes.
And see Nothing.
And now open that body's eyes and recognize that that Nothing is appearing as everything.
It's only that human mind that judges It as good or bad,
as here or there.
It's still Nothing.
Close that body's eyes again and show me how Nothing feels.
Don't try to describe It.
Don't try to feel It.
Let go of everything and feel what's left when you're not trying to feel,
when you're not trying to see, when you're not trying to understand.

One of Joel Goldsmith's living students, Virginia Stephenson (a centenarian at the time of this publication), said, "Learn to sit in the silence, knowing that there is an Interpreter within you higher than human judgment. This Interpreter is the healing Christ love, the Spirit of God in us, the I of our being. As we let the I function, we see the real more clearly as the shadows of material sense disappear in the light of truth. Then we can say, 'Oh, yes, Christ walks the earth today just as much as It did two thousand years ago as Jesus. The selfsame Spirit that multiplied the loaves and the fishes and raised up Jesus from the dead is here and operating now as this continuous living link of Love.'"

It created you. It's sustaining you. It has healed you.
You're thinking as Me now. That's why it's so quiet (t)here.
That's why your attention is so sharp there.
Like a razor's edge,
It's cutting through the illusion that you're not good enough,
that it's too late,
that it won't happen,
but you have to consolidate.
Notice how many things you desire during the day,
how many things you desire in an hour.
And that's why you don't see a single one.
You have to desire only one thing,
knowing I am here,
hearing my Name.
Every time a desire comes,
chant, hear, feel, and you will see it appearing:
My Name, My Breath, My Feeling is the answered prayer.
It's the sign of things to come.
Things that are already here that come into view.
I've made all things new,
but to get to that next part of your life,
you have to die to this part.
You have to not react to this part,
not desire or want in this part,
just chant and be happy.
You have to be Baba now.

You have to be the Christ now.
You have to be the Mother now.
You don't become.
Affirm: Whatever I can become is not who I am.
I am that I am.
I am what I am.

Nirvana Shatakam

BY SHANKARA

Translated from Sanskrit by Ivan M. Granger

I am not mind, not intellect, not ego, not thought.
I am not the ears, the tongue, the nose or the eyes,
   or what they witness,
I am neither earth nor sky, not air nor light.
I am knowledge and bliss.
I am Shiva! I am Shiva!
I am not the breath of prana, nor its five currents.
I am not the seven elements, nor the five organs,
Nor am I the voice or hands or anything that acts.
I am knowledge and bliss.
I am Shiva! I am Shiva!
I have no hatred or preference, neither greed nor
   desire nor delusion.
Pride, conflict, jealousy—these have no part of me.
Nothing do I own, nothing do I seek, not even liberation itself.
I am knowledge and bliss.
I am Shiva! I am Shiva!
I know neither virtue nor vice, neither pleasure nor pain.
I know no sacred chants, no holy places, no scriptures, no
   rituals.
I know neither the taste nor the taster.
I am knowledge and bliss.
I am Shiva! I am Shiva!
I fear not death. I doubt neither my being nor my place.

I have no father or mother; I am unborn.

I have no relatives, no friends. I have no guru and
no devotees.

I am knowledge and bliss.

I am Shiva! I am Shiva!

Free from doubt, I am formless.

With knowledge, in knowledge, I am everywhere,
beyond perception.

I am always the same. Not free, not trapped—I am.

I am knowledge and bliss.

I am Shiva! I am Shiva!

Truly, I am Shiva, pure awareness.

Shivo Ham! Shivo Ham!

PART FOUR

Spreading Love

"When we Love God, it's not just for Him; it's for everyone."

SISTER GRAZIELLE OF GALILEE

"Lord Ram gave Hanuman a quizzical look and said, 'What are you, a monkey or a man?' Hanuman bowed his head reverently, folded his hands and said, 'When I do not know who I am, I serve You and when I do know who I am, You and I are One.'"

TULSIDAS, *RAMCHARITMANAS*

"Let this mind be in you which was also in Christ Jesus, who, being in the form of God, did not consider it robbery to be equal with God, but made Himself of no reputation, taking the form of a bondservant, and coming in the likeness of men. And being found in appearance as a man, He humbled Himself and became obedient to the point of death, even the death of the cross."

PHILIPPIANS 2:5-8, NKJV

"Listen,
Stand up in prayer during the night,
For you are a candle,
And at night,
A candle stands and burns."

A SUFI SAYING

And when you believe in this world (as something separate
or other than God),
it is the night.
It is the Kali Yuga (the age of ignorance).
And the Kali Upanishad says that to go from night to day,
to go from ignorance to enlightenment,
you stand and chant.
You stand and sing.
You stand and praise,
in the dark,
in the storm.
You stand knowing,
God is Here.
Love is Here.
The Dawn is Here.
Even when we can't see It,
we feel It.
We thank It.
For everything.

"Lord, make me an instrument of your peace.

Where there is hatred, let me sow love;

where there is injury, pardon;

where there is doubt, faith;

where there is despair, hope;

where there is darkness, light;

and where there is sadness, joy.

O Divine Master, grant that I may not so much seek

to be consoled as to console;

to be understood as to understand;

to be loved as to love.

For it is in giving that we receive;

it is in pardoning that we are pardoned;

and it is in dying that we are born to eternal life.

Amen."

———————

ATTRIBUTED TO SAINT FRANCIS OF ASSISI

Silently Bless Everyone You Meet

Tenderness is our nature.

Love is our nature.

Service is our nature.

Blessings are our responsibility.

THE QUOTE

"If God is the center of your life, no words are necessary. Your mere presence will touch hearts."

―――――――

SAINT VINCENT DE PAUL

THE PRACTICE

Silently bless everyone you meet on your path.

Feel Love inside while you look at people.

Feel the Love that you are, where you see people.

Be still and know (feel) the Kingdom of Love where the eyes register the world.

I find that holding "others" in the Light keeps "me" in the Light, consciously. This Light dissolves the concepts of "other" and "me" ... revealing the Truth that right where we appear to be, there's only this Light, shining. Only this One Light. Just One Love appearing as you, as me, as everything.

Love is feeling God inside and then being It in the world, being Love in the world, standing in Love, standing as Love for everyone. Saint Vincent de Paul's quote has always resonated with me because I do my best every morning to find words to express that which I know can't be put into words. Truly, it doesn't matter what I say. It doesn't matter, really, what you hear; it's what you feel. And I know you can feel me because otherwise you wouldn't still be reading, listening, drawn. You can feel your Self when you're reading these words. I'm just the pen, the microphone, the doorway, a mirror.

I'm your mirror pointing you back to your Self,
so you can have a good look at your Self,
a good feel of your Self,
and then I send you out into the world for you to keep feeling
your Self while you're interacting with the world.
Your Self,
your Love.

God has to be more real to you than the chair you're sitting in.
It has to be more real to you than the trees you see,
than the cars that come past.
You have to feel Love while your eyes see the world.
While your mind thinks its thoughts, you have to feel Love.
You have to keep some attention in your Self
And on your Self.
Not that body, not that mind; attention needs to be on attention.
Attend to (t)His Love.

Notice how you can move your attention from the words on this page to the feeling of your breath in your nostrils, to the loudest sound you can hear in your environment, and to the softest, quietest sound. Attention isn't a mysterious concept. Where is your attention now? God is saying, "Keep it on Me." Keep it on the silence, on the Love, until there's no difference between your attention and Love. Your attention becomes Love. The healing agent. The miracle worker. The divine intervention. No words needed . . . except "Thank you."

Your body is appearing in this ocean of Love that you are. Your body is just another object in the Self. The Self that is there is the same Self that is "here." The same Self is manifesting as India and all the people there, as China and all the people there, as Africa and all the people there. And as long as you're in touch with that Essence, that Substance, you have nothing to worry about. The body that you're aware of will be taken care of. Its needs will be taken care of. That's why the Bible says you shouldn't even take thought for what you'll wear or what you'll eat. You stay with the Love. It doesn't think.

Don't worry.

Trust.

> ## "Trust deeper."
>
> ---
>
> ### DR. SADEGHI, TO ME BEFORE THE
> ### SOUTH AFRICA TRIP WHEN I MET OPRAH

This week, wherever you find yourself, I want you to silently bless every person who crosses your path. Every person you see, you feel Love while you're looking at them. That's the blessing. You don't have to say,

"Bless you, my darling," or "Bless you, Beloved." You don't have to do any of that. You just see the person but feel their Substance, their Reality, their Truth, and so it's like you're looking at them through the eyes of Love. Looking at them feelingly. You're holding them in Loving-kindness, every single person, and you're going to forget.

I look, whether at a person or an object, often without blinking, until the shift occurs. I go from seeing the surface to feeling the depths. What I'm seeing doesn't change, but my knowing does. It's a shift from being a person looking at another person or object, to being Love aware of Itself everywhere and nowhere.

You're going to forget, and you're going to keep forgetting. But that one time you remember, you're going to want to jump up and down for joy because you're going to finally see the truth that, oh, these are not humans walking around. This is God in drag, as Ram Dass would say, showing up looking like people, but it's just God here. Only God is here. Only Love is here. That was my mantra. It's still my mantra, really, just wordlessly. The mother of Sahaja Yoga, Nirmala Devi, called it "thought-less awareness." Only Love is here, and It knows that, is That, so there's no need to announce or repeat it. I see people, a lot of people, but there's only One here. There's only one Self appearing as "here" and as the many, and I am That, and so are you. And so, just your knowing this, going out among the seeming people, is your true work. That's your true purpose.

If you have been enjoying the words that come from me and the feel-ing that you find when you hear me, then your true purpose is knowing and being this wherever you are and knowing that what is yours will come to you, will find you. Your outer purpose, your work, your abundance, your relationships, will all come to you, will find you, as long as you're liv-ing in this truth and knowing this truth for all the seeming others.

I find that practicing holding others in the Light keeps me in the Light consciously, which brings that felt-knowing that there's only the Light, only one Light. The Light I feel here seemingly inside and as Nikki is the

Light that I know is everywhere. Just one Love appearing as you, appearing as me, appearing as everything.

I repeat myself often so that if this message slips past your conscious mind, you'll hear it for the first time again. You'll feel It. You will again remember that you wrote this book and placed it in this seeming dream, at this seeming time to wake up and begin.

Loving with No Brakes

THE QUOTES

"I am the Father of the world. The whole world is my child."

_____

MAHARAJJI

"If you want to be self-propelled, it is important to start by fixing your intention. Make your intention as all-encompassing as you can. Start with a simple resolve. Decide to be a Mother to the World. That means seeing everyone as your own. There is no one who is not part of your clan. When you walk down the street, are you capable of looking upon everyone with the same sweetness of emotion that arises within you when you see your child coming home from school? This intention alone could liberate you from much agitation and negativity and could have a tremendous impact on how you craft your destiny.

"If you are conscious every moment that everything and everyone on this planet is yours, you do not need any laws to tell you what you shall or shall not do. You have changed your fundamental identity. Your karmic boundaries now fall away and you experience a sense of boundlessness. A new identity of inclusiveness and involvement is born."

_____

SADHGURU

"For truly I tell you, if you have faith the size of a mustard seed, you can say to this mountain, 'Move from here to there,' and it will move. Nothing will be impossible for you."

———————

MATTHEW 17:20-21, BSB

THE PRACTICE

This week, you are the Mother, the Father, of the world. That's not your coworker, that's Love appearing as "coworker." That's your child. And even when you're mad at your child, that Love doesn't stop. Just for now, look at EVERYONE that way. Love everyone that way. Sweetly. With no brakes. With no breaks. With no conditions. With no "me," we Know Him, only.

Look around at the space you find that body in and remind yourself, this is Love appearing as this space.

This is God appearing as this room, as this body, as these thoughts, as these words that are telling you to "relax without laziness, focus without tension, perceive without projecting, witness without judging, love without condition, serve without self-seeking, meditate without identity, correct without blaming, guide without superiority." To "be without self-defining," to "be one with God." That's Mooji. He said, "The whole human thing, it doesn't work by itself. It only works when it is inside the heart and it meets God and you walk together first, and then you walk as one." You sit as one. God appearing as you seated, God appearing as you smiling, as you remembering, as your faith returns. It was right here all along, but you've turned to It again.

Whenever you're scared, you're projecting out into the future. You're overwhelmed. You have to turn this way. You have to remember to feel This, just a little bit of It. Christ told us that we need only faith the size of a mustard seed to move our mountains. We just have to feel this Love a little bit. We have to wake up out of the drama long enough to recognize that only Love is here. This is Love appearing as drama, and It's appearing as drama only because I forgot Love.

A beautiful way to intend not to forget, a beautiful way to stay turned, is to decide to be a mother to the world or a father to the world.

Even when you're mad at your child, you never stop feeling Love for them. You can start with that simple resolve, seeing everyone as your own, like there's no one who is not a part of your clan. Everyone is your person, your people, your crew.

> "There is nothing outside of yourself that ever can enable you to get better, stronger, richer, quicker, or smarter. Everything is within."
>
> ———————
>
> **MIYAMOTO MUSASHI,** *THE BOOK OF FIVE RINGS*

And what you have to do, as Robert Browning said, *is "open out a way for this imprisoned splendor to escape."* You have to hear so you can See. You have to Feel to see through the veil.

Close that body's eyes in a moment,
and make God contact, again.
Become more sensitive to this Love.
Touch this Love.
When you're feeling It in every breath and every step,
feeling It before you fall asleep at night,
turning to It as soon as you regain consciousness in the morning,
as soon as you become aware,
before those eyes even open in the morning,
feeling This,
feeling Him,

recognizing that you're in God and She's in you,
that all the power is in you,
that there is no other power,
as long as you're feeling This,
you're covered.
You're under the Mantle,
under the Blanket,
under His Wing.
When you're not feeling This,
when you stop feeling This,
you're like Simon Peter in the Bible
when Jesus called him out onto the water.
He was standing on the water, too.
He started looking around.
He started getting scared.
He started doubting, and he started sinking.
He went under.
When you're feeling this Love,
you're walking on water in every step.
You're knowing who you are in every step.
Your eyes are fixed on Him.
You never take your eyes off this Love that's beyond
whatever it is you're looking at.
You're feeling the Love beyond it,
beyond them,
or you're seeing them and knowing they're your child.
They're yours, and you Love them so much.
How would that change your day? Your week? Your life?
You don't have to say this to them (but sometimes it does
look like a conversation, or a smile, or a compliment—
Love unfolds naturally),

but you always feel It powerfully.
That's not your coworker.
That's Love appearing as your coworker.
That's your child, just for now.
Look at everyone that way.
That'll help you feel into the Love that's behind,
that's beyond them,
that existed before they appeared,
the Love that existed before you appeared.
When we keep rising,
we drop even that identity,
the one that considers itself mother or father.
We go beyond all identities,
beyond all names,
to the nameless one that's calling our names.
Can you hear It?
All you need is a quiet mind.

The Indian philosopher and teacher Sri Aurobindo said, "A quiet mind does not mean that there will be no thoughts or mental movements at all, but that these will be on the surface and you will feel your true being within separate from them, observing but not carried away."

Focused without tension, being without defining, loving with no brakes. I love you and I'm with you, and what you're going through, we'll get through together, as the One.

Discovering the
Sweetness of Alignment

Everything is as it should be for you to become in time what you already have always been. God became man that man might become God. Stay on your throne this week. Sit up taller today. Breathe deeper in this moment as you hear Love's Silence, holding Its Vibration inside. Feel it. Go right to It. Don't try. Don't listen to the thought that says, "But Nikki, I can't feel It. I can't. I don't know what you're talking about." Those are just thoughts that are seeming to cover up (t)His Vibration. Just go right to the Vibration, whether you feel It in the feet, or in the legs, or in the stomach, or in the chest. Breathe into that Feeling like you blow on an incense stick and see it light up bright orange. Breathe into It and It seems to grow. Don't let go of That. Let go of everything else but That. Thoughts come and your attention goes there. Notice that and breathe back into the One, into the Truth, into your Self. Come alive and stay alive. Everything is working for you, to uplift you, to support your growth. Everything and everyone, even the bitter ones, even the angry ones, even the seemingly unhelpful ones, it's all for your benefit. Keep catching them and smiling at them, knowing that they are not them. They are Him, and because you and the Father are one, they are you. And do you have your best interest at heart?

THE QUOTES

"Now I knew the meaning of the words '*The Kingdom of God is within you.*' . . . I noted that interior prayer bears fruit in three ways: in the Spirit, in the feelings, and in revelations. In the first, for instance, is the sweetness of the love of God, inward peace, gladness of mind, purity of thought, and the sweet remembrance of God. In the second, the pleasant warmth of the heart, fullness of delight in all one's limbs, the joyous 'bubbling' in the heart, lightness and courage, the joy of living, power not to feel sickness and sorrow."

———————

THE WAY OF A PILGRIM

"Once you cultivate Equanimity within, every cell in your body will respond by generating Sweetness."

———————

SADHGURU

"Essentially, what you are seeking is an ultimate sense of sweetness within you. Either you hit it accidentally or consciously—that is the choice you have."

———————

SADHGURU

"Look past your thoughts, so you may drink the pure nectar of this moment."

———————

ATTRIBUTED TO RUMI

THE PRACTICE

Feel the inner Sweetness and then do something sweet for someone. Let that sweetness take the form of a GoOD deed!

I was watching myself on a recording the other day. I'm not a fan of watching myself on anything (unless I'm watching myself watching!). I try not to, but sometimes I have to if the production team wants feedback. I noticed that when I went from doing the talking points that were needed to make the video happen, to go from that, to shifting into just the way I talk on the podcast every morning, I began to sway. This body began rocking and swaying its way into the conscious awareness of this Sweetness. I could see just when I remembered, or just when It announced itself where I was, and there I went swaying. It was very gentle. I'm sure if you watched it, you'd be very aware of what was happening. Maybe someone else would think it was a nervous habit, but it was beautiful. As soon as I saw the sway, I began swaying in that moment as I watched myself and listened.

But that word "Sweetness," that's the word I could hear as I watched myself on that video swaying. This Love has often been called Sweetness in many places; many authors, many saints, have described it as a nectar or a honey.

"The sweetness of life, the relaxed presence is the perfume of our essence, our no self. This nectar is natural. It is life itself. From this nectar everything good grows in our being and in our life. Remembering our no self is to remember this nectar, life's inherent sweetness."

DR. BRUCE DAVIS, *THE CALLING OF JOY!*

Let's practice feeling that Sweetness now;
in a moment, close that body's eyes.
And imagine that I am standing behind you with a big
Winnie the Pooh vat,
an enormous bucket of honey.
But it's not your typical honey.
It's not something you can touch.
It's not sticky,
and you can't taste it with that human tongue,
but it is sweet.
You can think of it like, "I have a big bucket of Light,
and I am beginning right now to pour It right there into
the top of your head,
this Light."
Just like honey pours,
this flow is uninterrupted.
It's rich and full.

As I pour It at the crown of your head,
It flows down into your heart and you can feel It.
You can feel this Light as the Sweetness.
You can feel the Love It is.
An unending flow from your crown to your heart that makes
that face smile.
It makes your whole being Sweet.
Later, the same Sweetness is going to sweeten your actions.
You'll notice that you want to be of service.
You want to help.
You want to see how you can help "others."
The way you feel right now,
this True Self that you're aware of right now,
is what makes you go out and treat others as your Self.

Notice that with eyes open,
looking around the room that you're in from this Sweetness,
from Love,
from this Honey,
this Nectar,
everything that you're aware of is this sweet Light in form.
You're noticing that there is nothing that you can be aware of that
is not This.
Everything is the Sweetness,
and when you feel It,
you feel good.
You feel God.
Each day this week, do something nice for someone.
It could be to pay a compliment to a stranger.
It could be to hold the door for somebody,
to hold the elevator for someone,
to send a sweet email to a coworker.
Just a note of gratitude.
It could be to make a phone call to someone who keeps coming into
your awareness.
It could be to sit right where you are and feel Love where thoughts
of the world,
or specific people, are.
Send them healing, abundance, peace.

Whatever you pray for for others, you automatically receive.

Do something kind and allow that to deepen your awareness, your experience of this goodness, this Godness right where you are.

PART FIVE

The Fruit of Love

Eternal Dawn

Rumi said, "The breeze at dawn has secrets to tell you. Don't go
back to sleep."
It's always dawn Here,
and you're awake,
and you know the Secret now.
And you'll share It with just a glance;
just your sight blesses.
They call it Darshan in India.
You're not just one in the crowd anymore.
You are the crowd.
And so when you see your other selves, bless them.
"May you be healthy,
may you be happy.
May you be whole.
May you be at peace."
And you're wanting that for them because they are you, too.
They're Him.
They're all your children.
You're genuinely wanting that for that seeming stranger.

And because you've named that desire in your heart for them,
because you want that for them,
you get it, too.
You receive it, too.
Focus not on yourself
but on your Self.
You have to stay focused in the Spirit,
on God,
or as God appearing as others.
Remember, that's what Maharajji said makes you a saint.
The moment you focus on yourself,
sainthood is lost,
and you are a saint,
and you've got work to do.

Your Practice
Will Bear Fruit Quickly

Usually I'm up at 5:00 a.m.
During this past month and a half,
I've been up experimenting with 3:00,
even 2:30, in the morning.
I've found that as long I do some practice at night before bed,
I don't need an alarm clock.
My body naturally rises before the sun, and 4:00 a.m. seems
to be the sweet spot.
As I was rising earlier and deepening further in Love,
I had a dream.
I was at a family event,
like a wedding reception.
And the energy was high,
the volume level was high.
I remember turning to the table right next to mine,
to the seat closest to mine at that next table,
and finding my Grandpa Robert there,
smiling at me, beaming.
He transitioned when I was sixteen and left his final words,
"Watch Nikki," as a message of instruction for me, later.
As my highest practice.

The Supreme Yoga.

And so I look over,

I see him,

and he is beaming,

he is twinkling,

he is shining.

And there was the conscious thought,

"You are not supposed to be here . . .

I don't even know what we're doing, or where we're at . . .

but you are not supposed to be here."

And he started speaking in what was not English.

Through my big smile,

I said, "Grandpa, I can't understand you."

And then he started speaking slower and almost in a labored way.

In the dream, it felt like he was speaking Spanish,

but in hindsight it may have been Hindi.

But the English words he gave to me were,

"You have to prune the branches," or

"Your branches are being pruned,"

and that's it.

But there was so much Love.

When I noticed him,

he was already looking at me.

He was already smiling at me,

waiting for me to recognize him,

waiting for me to receive that message.

And for a month, I didn't quite understand what that meant.

And then I came to John 15 again.

I could feel John 15 bubbling up in me.

As you continue reading the following words, take your right palm

and face it up toward the sky (elbow bent).

Sit up tall,

straight,
not strained,
comfortably tall,
with your feet rooted on the floor.
No matter if you're on the third floor,
the twentieth floor,
or the ground floor, you're rooted in Love.
Rooted in the Ground of Being.
You're breathing in Love.
Holding the book with your left hand,
take that right hand,
palm facing up, like you are receiving this Love,
like your arm is a branch.

Receive this message while you receive this God flow
as if through that hand.
Jesus said, "I am the true Vine and my Father is the Worker.
Whichever branch that does not produce fruit by Me, He cuts it off.
And the one that produces fruit, He prunes it, so that it brings
much fruit." (John 15:1–2, in Victor N. Alexander, Aramaic Scripture)

That's what you've been feeling.
If you've been feeling stuck or frustrated,
if you've been feeling thwarted,
like things aren't happening the way you want them to happen,
or feel like you need them to happen,
if it feels like you're not,
your projects are not producing fruit, hear me.
You are the fruit.
You are also technically the branch and the leaves and the tree,
but you are the fruit.
Not money,

not how many clients or followers you have,
or customers or projects or new contracts.
Those appear to be the fruit,
But you are the fruit.
This Presence that you are is the fruit,
Even if it's just for seconds at a time,
and sprinkled into the more frequent moments of fear and anxiety,
that Peace that comes, that rises in you,
His Peace that rises in you,
that Joy that rises up like the sap,
that Faith that comes that does not judge by appearances,
that's the fruit.
Even your faith right now is being pruned so that you may have
more faith.
So those are not the pains of failure or the pains of lack.
These are the pains of abundance.
You're not being punished;
you're being pruned.
This is a minor pain you must bear right now,
in this season, because this fruit that you are is about to get heavier.
It's about to become ripe.
That's one thing Krishna Das told me when I visited him for the day
earlier this year.
We were talking about the Bible, specifically the New Testament,
and how oftentimes it's interpreted as Jesus talking about good
versus evil.
But Krishna Das had been studying Aramaic, too,
the language that Jesus spoke during the time he walked the Earth.
And he had also read Neil Douglas-Klotz's Revelations of the
Aramaic Jesus,
and he said, "Nikki, Jesus wasn't saying good and evil.
He was saying ripe and unripe; we have to be ripe fruit."

You've bloomed.
In our weeks together,
our practicing together,
your flower has opened,
but now you're fruiting.
Maybe you were unripe when we started,
but right now it's like
you're in the sun,
and it's paradoxical, because it's going to appear that you will
ripen in time,
in your own time.
But in any given Holy Instant,
either you are ripe or you are unripe.
And right now, you are ripe because I can feel you receiving the Son,
receiving this Word as if through that palm,
as if through those eyes and ears,
because you've been given ears to hear this message—
my words,
but it's His Word that vibrates between them, that's vibrating as them.

You're hearing My words inside,
but you're also hearing the Silence that they're coming from.
You have to hear everyone's words like that
to hear what they're really meaning.
To know what's really here constantly is only Love,
even though it appears to be breathing,
talking, walking, working, crying and laughing.
Can you stay aware of the Essence, the Substance, the Sap?
Jesus said, "And the one that produces fruit, He prunes it, so that it
brings much fruit.
You are already cleansed, because of the Milta [the manifestation or
the Word]

I presented you.

Graft yourselves onto me, and I onto you,

for the branch cannot bring fruit by itself, if it is not grafted to the vine;

likewise you also, if you do not adhere to me.

I am the vine and you are the branches.

Whoever adheres to me and I to them,

they shall bring much fruit.

Because without me,

you cannot do anything.

For if a person does not adhere to me,

they are cast out. Like a branch that withers,

[which] they cut off and throw into the fire to burn.

And for those of you who adhere to me and my words take hold in you,

whatever you wish to ask for,

you shall have.

By this the Father is glorified,

that you bear plentiful fruit. And that you become my disciples.

Just as my Father has loved me,

I too shall love you.

Nourish [yourselves] with my love." (John 15:2–9, in Victor N. Alexander, Aramaic Scripture)

"There is no greater love."

JESUS (JOHN 15:13),
VICTOR N. ALEXANDER, ARAMAIC SCRIPTURE

Your practice will bear fruit quickly as long as you sit at least twice a day in the Son—thirty minutes in the morning upon rising, preferably before the sun rises, and thirty minutes in the evening before bedtime. You can sit comfortably on the floor or in a chair, no particular posture is necessary, and hold your palms open and facing upward (elbows bent), receiving Love, giving Love. Being Love. Note: The Son feels less harsh than the sun. It's not an intense heat; it's a cool Light, a soothing, calming, tender Radiance, more akin to the moon.

Eventually, you stop being the one whose palms are up.

You stop being the one who's smiling.

You stop being the one who's sitting up straighter into the Silence.

You start being the Silence Itself.

You recognize that you're the Love Itself.

The Love you're trying to feel right now is what You are.

You can't leave the Silence.

There's no thought that can distract you from your Self.

That can make you not be your Self,

or more of your Self.

You are your Self even while you appear to be the one who has all the problems.

The one who's getting older,

the one who's afraid,

who worries about everything.

Let her worry.

Let him worry.

That's what it does.

But you be the Fixer.

The Forgiver,

the Healer.

That's what this Consciousness that You are, is.

A Note from Love to Love

> "Also you shall testify, that from the beginning
> You have been with me."
>
> ――――――
>
> JESUS (JOHN 15:27),
> VICTOR N. ALEXANDER, ARAMAIC SCRIPTURE

You have been with Love since the beginning.
Love is Jesus's real Name,
His hidden Name.
It's your real Name,
your hidden Name.
It's the Father's Name.
The Mother's Name.

If your arm is tired from holding your right palm up,
you can rest it upward on your knee.
But notice the seeming difference when you're using that body as
an antenna.
Using that arm (once you put the book down, you'll hold both
palms this way)

like a branch,
especially if you flex your palm as if to arch it up toward the ceiling
or the sky,
feel how much more aware of the Love you are.
Just that little bit of tension in your hand—you can feel the
contrast.
God puts a little bit of tension in your life so you can feel the
contrast,
so that you seek Him.
Your outstretched hand is not causing you to feel more Love,
but in the beginning of this practice,
an extra bit of effort brings on the effortless,
seemingly faster.
Now, place your right palm out in front of you
(the back of your hand toward you),
as if you're giving Love.
As if you're giving a blessing now.
Years ago, I had a very vivid,
lucid dream of just my hand out in front of me.
And there was a beautiful veil—
transparent and silky in texture, that I was caressing.
It was purplish-blue in hue.
And on the other side of that veil,
which was blowing in a wind
that didn't feel like a physical wind,
on the other side was another hand.
It was Baba Ram Dass's hand.
And I never saw his face.
I just knew it was his hand,
and we were touching palms with that veil between,
and it was so beautiful.

"There was a saint named Gyaneshwar who lived in the 1200s,
and he said, "The Kundalini, as she uncoils herself in you,
she then reaches the palms of the hands creating a draft.
A life wind emerges and creates a cooling sensation internally
as well as externally."

NIRMALA DEVI, *THE BREEZE OF SAHASRARA*

As you become more sensitive to this Love,
as you become God sensitive,
you're going to begin to feel vibrations on your palms.
You're going to begin to feel a coolness there,
even if your body is warm,
as a way to know that you are open,
as a way of knowing only Love is here.
Say that confidently: "Only the fullness of Love is here.
And I'm that Love."

As you go out into your day,
into your life,
as you're driving the car,
keep your right (or left) palm open on your thigh.
Keep it facing heaven as often as you can.
When you're listening to anything,
scrolling with your left hand,
have that right palm open to Love,
receiving and giving and sensing,
feeling for a cooling sensation,
a breeze,
Her breath,
the Holy Spirit moving in the midst of you.

I'm very blessed to be in the midst of you. When your hand is out and open to Love, it's out and open to me. Mine is out and open to you.

I Love you
I'm with you
I Am You

Nik

A Note on Forgiveness

If you're having a challenging time becoming aware of,
sustaining,
being,
and spreading Love,
it is because there's a belief present that you are guilty,
unworthy,
or need to forgive yourself or others.
Right where that thought is, the state of Forgiveness is.
Those thoughts of "I am not there yet"
are sounding,
appearing in the always-present state of Forgiveness.
Sit back up into Forgiveness, into the remembrance of Truth.
The Mind can't think at this altitude.
It's quiet up Here.

You know you're back Here
because you'll be smiling,
knowing,
still, again.
The thoughts dissolve.
Silence reigns.
The state of Forgiveness is the constant awareness of Love,
of God.
Only Christ can forgive.
You have to be(come) That to recognize that there is no one here to
forgive,
and no one to do the forgiving.
Only Love is here, and in this,
nothing ever happened.
The past is a thought.
Thoughts are as real as the dream you had five years ago.

"You see the world
And you try to dissolve it.
But the master has no need to.
He is without desire.
For though he sees,
He sees nothing."

THE HEART OF AWARENESS:
A TRANSLATION OF THE ASHTAVAKRA GITA

"Forgiveness recognizes what you thought your brother did to you has not occurred. It does not pardon sins and make them real. It sees there was no sin. And in that view are all your sins forgiven. What is sin, except a false idea about God's Son? Forgiveness merely sees its falsity, and therefore lets it go. What then is free to take its place is now the Will of God."

—————

A COURSE IN MIRACLES

"I am upset because I see something that is not there."

—————

A COURSE IN MIRACLES

You Are the Prayer

First, you wake up to Love.
Then, you learn to watch life while feeling Love.
Finally, you wake up as Love,
being a reflection of It in the world,
serving and spreading Love to the rest of the reflection.

"In my world love is the only law. I do not ask for love, I give it."

———

NISARGADATTA MAHARAJ

"And if you understand that, you will understand that you didn't finish reading this book, you finished writing it."

———

ATTRIBUTED TO JED McKENNA

"Rama,
there are four gate-keepers at the entrance to the Realm of
Freedom, moksha.
They are
self-control,

spirit of enquiry,

contentment and

good company.

The wise seeker should diligently cultivate the friendship of

these, or at least one of them."

YOGA VASISTHA

"When you know you are part of the divine plan, you stop demanding. Then you know everything is being done for you."

SRI SRI RAVI SHANKAR

"You are lost only because you are searching."

U. G. KRISHNAMURTI

"Mind creates the abyss, the heart crosses it."

NISARGADATTA MAHARAJ

We've been walking down the path of contentment together since Week 1,
meeting GoOD company along the way,
meeting challenges from the feeling of contentment,
facing every challenge with a smile,
never lost because we're not searching,
not demanding because everything is being done for us, through us, by us.
Close your eyes and breathe into your Heart.

That Heart at the top of your head,
in the space directly above where your head appears to be.
Breathe into that Heart like It's an ember that you're causing to
glow brighter and brighter with every exhale.
You're feeling Love stronger.
It's lighting up that face now.
It's lighting up those cells.

Every inch of your being is glowing; your Consciousness is radiat-
ing the God within.
The Indian spiritual teacher Papaji said, "God lives inside you,
and you live inside God."
You live in the Kingdom.
That's why contentment is your natural state.
Just as health is the natural state of your body,
contentment is the natural state of your mind.
Bliss, this ever-permanent, unchanging Love that's glowing as your body,
is the essence of your Soul, your experience of your inherent health
as God-given contentment.
The glow of your spirit changes your experience of Now.
It's changing your experience of what we call "the Present."
It's changing your experience of what you call "work."
It's changing your experience of what you call "you."
Call it all Love.
"Now," or "Here," or "this moment" are just names we call God.
Sometimes, we call It "Monday."
Sometimes, we call it "yesterday."
Sometimes, we call it "next year,"
but it's only (t)His presence that you're never not experiencing.
Any work you do is happening for God.
It's happening in God while you're remembering God, feeling God.
Only God is here, God in various seeming forms.

But It's all just your Self.

That body that's breathing,

whose heart is beating,

who is listening to these words seemingly inside,

is God appearing, the same one God you keep meeting on

this path of contentment.

Every seeming person you bump into,

every stranger, every child . . .

They look in your direction as if to say, "Can you see me?

Do you know who I am?"

Practice remembering who you are and who I am.

Practice knowing that you're in GoOD company always.

It's all the Self.

That's the true meaning of contentment.

It's all the Self,

all you.

There's nothing to desire.

It's all yours.

You just forgot.

In that forgetfulness, you suffer.

When it's all you, there's no one to be jealous of, or to hate, or to fear,

only Love to recognize.

It can't be given.

It can't be received.

It's just experienced from moment to seeming moment.

With every step along the path and every breath we turn

toward Love,

we breathe into Love.

We glow as Love.

In that glowing,

we recognize that there were never steps.

There were never breaths.

There was never anyone to turn toward Love or to practice Love,
to recognize Love.
There's only Love.
Only Love is.
And that's the final Truth.

"If I make use of the tongues of men and of angels,

and have not love,

I am like sounding brass,

or a loud-tongued bell.

And if I have a prophet's power,

and have knowledge of all secret things;

and if I have all faith,

by which mountains may be moved from their place,

but have not love,

I am nothing.

And if I give all my goods to the poor,

and if I give my body to be burned,

but have not love,

it is of no profit to me.

Love is never tired of waiting;

Love is kind;

love has no envy;

love has no high opinion of itself,

love has no pride;

Love's ways are ever fair,

it takes no thought for itself;

it is not quickly made angry,

it takes no account of evil;

It takes no pleasure in wrongdoing,

but has joy in what is true;
Love has the power of undergoing all things,
having faith in all things, hoping all things.
Though the prophet's word may come to an end,
tongues come to nothing,
and knowledge have no more value,
love has no end.
For our knowledge is only in part,
and the prophet's word gives only a part of what is true:
But when that which is complete is come,
then that which is in part will be no longer necessary.
When I was a child,
I made use of a child's language,
I had a child's feelings
and a child's thoughts:
now that I am a man,
I have put away the things of a child.
For now we see things in a glass, darkly;
but then face to face:
now my knowledge is in part;
then it will be complete,
even as God's knowledge of me.
But now we still have faith, hope, love, these three; and the
greatest of these is love."

———————

1 CORINTHIANS 13:1-13, BBE

You are the Revelation.
You are the Prayer,
answered.

Love Appearing As My Favorite Books

Aramaic Scripture: New Testament Translated from the Ancient Aramaic Language by Victor N. Alexander

Ashtavakra Gita

Autobiography of a Yogi by Paramhansa Yogananda

Be As You Are: The Teachings of Sri Ramana Maharshi

Be Love Now by Ram Dass

Beyond Happiness: Finding and Fulfilling Your Deepest Desire by Frank J. Kinslow

Bhagavad Gita

A Book of God's Love by M. R. Bawa Muhaiyaddeen

By His Grace: A Devotee's Story by Dada Mukerjee

Celebrating Silence by Sri Sri Ravi Shankar

Chants of a Lifetime: Searching for a Heart of Gold by Krishna Das

A Course in Miracles by Foundation for Inner Peace

A Course in Miracles Made Easy: Mastering the Journey from Fear to Love by Alan Cohen

Eufeeling! The Art of Creating Inner Peace and Outer Prosperity by Frank J. Kinslow

Falling into Grace: Insights on the End of Suffering by Adyashanti

From and for God: Collected Poetry and Writings on the Spiritual Path by Sitaram Dass

Fullness of Joy: A Spiritual Guide to the Paradise Within by John Stephenson

I Am That by Nisargadatta Maharaj

The Infinite Way by Joel Goldsmith

The Interior Castle by Saint Teresa of Avila

The Interlinear Bible: Hebrew-Greek-English (English, Hebrew and Greek Edition)

It All Abides in Love: Maharajji Neem Karoli Baba by Jai Ram Ransom

The Jap Ji: The Message of Guru Nanak by Kirpal Singh

Joy 24 x 7: Jeetendra Jain Explores Joy with Sadhguru by Jaggi Vasudev

Living the Infinite Way by Joel Goldsmith

Living the Jesus Prayer by Irma Zaleski

Love Everyone: The Transcendent Wisdom of Neem Karoli Baba Told Through the Stories of the Westerners Whose Lives He Transformed by Parvati Markus

Ma in Her Words by Anandamayi Ma

Miracle of Love: Stories About Neem Karoli Baba by Ram Dass

Monastery Without Walls: Daily Life in the Silence by Bruce Davis

The Nag Hammadi Scriptures, edited by Marvin Meyer

One Hundred and Eight Questions: Answers to Calm Our Deepest Concerns by Shri Mataji Nirmala Devi

On Having No Head by Douglas Harding

Padamalai—Teachings of Sri Ramana Maharshi by Muruganar and David Godman

The Path of the Masters by Julian Johnson

Polishing the Mirror by Ram Dass

The Power of Now: A Guide to Spiritual Enlightenment by Eckhart Tolle

The Practice of the Presence of God by Brother Lawrence

A Return to Love by Marianne Williamson

Revelations of the Aramaic Jesus: The Hidden Teachings on Life and Death by Neil Douglas-Klotz

The Secret of the Rosary by St. Louis De Montfort

The Secret of Mary by St. Louis De Montfort

Silence of the Heart: Dialogues with Robert Adams by Robert Adams

Simple Peace: The Spiritual Life of St. Francis of Assisi by Bruce Davis

Stillness Speaks by Eckhart Tolle

St. Seraphim of Sarov by Valentine Zander

The Supreme Yoga: Yoga Vasistha by Swami Venkatesananda

The Transparency of Things: Contemplating the Nature of Experience by Rupert Spira

The Untethered Soul: The Journey Beyond Yourself by Michael A. Singer

The Way of the Rose: The Radical Path of the Divine Feminine Hidden in the Rosary by Clark Strand and Perdita Finn

What Am I? A Study in Non-Volitional Living by Galen Sharp

What's Wrong with Right Now? If You Don't Think About It by Sailor Bob Adamson

Who Am I? (Nan Yar?) by Sri Ramana Maharshi

The Wisdom of Sundays: Life-Changing Insights from Super Soul Conversations by Oprah Winfrey

Acknowledgments

I'm not a podcaster. I'm not an author. I'm a Servant. A GoOD Listener.

That's my lineage, my Origin.

Thank you, thank you, thank you to my children, Gia and Max, for your patience during my busy seasons and the inspired help you provided knowingly and unknowingly. Thank you, Gia, for allowing Love to use your hand to draw Love, on Love, for Love! Thank you, Mom and Dad, Elaine and Karl, for . . . EVERYTHING. I couldn't do any of this without your Love, support, and example. Thank you, Uncle BB, for your Divine Sight and wisdom. Thank you, Grandma Maxine, for teaching me; Syl, for inspiring me; Alex, for reminding me; KD, for singing to me; Raghu, for mic'ing me; Sheila, for rocking with me; Albany, for helping me; Perry, for snapping me; Jon, for pushing me; Sian-Ashleigh, for signing me; Judith, for seeing me; Gabi, for guiding me; Maharajji, for finding me; and Christ, for keeping me.

Thank YOU for reading Me.

I love you.

Credits

Many thanks to all the incredible spiritual teachers who are quoted in this book—for your inspiration and for permission to include your words.

Additional thanks and permissions are as follows:

Scripture quotations marked (AMP) are taken from the *Amplified Bible*, Copyright © 2015 by The Lockman Foundation. Used by permission.

Scripture quotations marked as BSB are taken from *The Holy Bible, Berean Study Bible, BSB*. Copyright © 2016, 2018 by Bible Hub. Used by permission. All rights reserved worldwide.

Scripture quotations marked ESV are taken from the ESV® Bible (*The Holy Bible, English Standard Version*®). Copyright © 2001 by Crossway, a publishing ministry of Good News Publishers. Used by permission. All rights reserved.

Scripture quotations marked MSG are taken from *THE MESSAGE*, copyright © 1993, 2002, 2018 by Eugene H. Peterson. Used by permission of NavPress. All rights reserved. Represented by Tyndale House Publishers, Inc.

Scripture texts used in this work are taken from the *New American Bible, revised edition* © 2010, 1991, 1986, 1970 by the Confraternity of Christian Doctrine, Washington, DC. Used by permission of the copyright owner. All rights reserved. No part of the *New American Bible* may be reproduced in any form without permission in writing from the copyright owner.

Scripture quotations marked NIV are taken from *The Holy Bible, New International Version*®, *NIV*®. Copyright © 1973, 1978, 1984, 2011 by Biblica, Inc.® Used by permission of Zondervan. All rights reserved worldwide. www.Zondervan.com. The "NIV" and "New International Version" are trademarks registered in the United States Patent and Trademark Office by Biblica, Inc.®

Scripture quotations marked NKJV are taken from the *New King James Version*®. Copyright © 1982 by Thomas Nelson. Used by permission. All rights reserved.